Think
& Act

LIKE A
WINNER

(An Indispensable Guide To Personal Performance)

R O B   W I L S O N

12-4-02

Library of Congress Cataloging — in — Publication Data

Wilson / Rob

Think & Act Like a Winner! / Rob Wilson

Includes biographical references and index.

ISBN   0-9710381-0-41. success   I Title

Manufactured in the United States of America 2001

Published by   Rob Wilson   A Million Miles of Motivation LLC. Publishing

400 Locust Street Ste. 253 Des Moines, IA 50309

To all the people who believed in me,

before I had the courage to believe in myself.

Excellence demands that you be better than yourself

~ Ted Engstrom

Table of Contents

Introduction

You were born to succeed. I believe that anyone who tells you differently is ignorant of this universal truth.

But make no mistake—success seldom arrives on a platter delivered directly to your table.

Those who adhere to certain universal principles, ageless laws that point the way to a richer and more satisfying life, achieve their desired goals and outcomes. The reason one individual succeeds where another one fails is that the successful person knows and applies these principles.

Have you ever found yourself wondering, "What am I going to be?" "Where will I be when I am older?" "Will I achieve great things, or is this it?" "Am I going to own my own company?" Will I stick with this company?" "Will I retire early?" "Will I have enough money . . . support . . .?"

It seems that some people have their lives all figured out, while others struggle to find answers to these questions.

When it comes to success, I have found that there are two types of people in this world. There are those who know exactly what it is they want to achieve and set everything in place to get it, and then there are those who are constantly grappling with themselves, and perhaps others around them, in an effort to find out what makes a person successful and how to achieve success.

My father used to tell me, "Rob, if you want to be a professional golfer, you have to hang out at the golf course, not the swimming pool. You might think that the swimming pool is more fun, but if you want to play golf well, you have to go where the pros play! They're out there on the course perfecting their game, day after day, sun up to sun down. Are you willing to do that, too?"

THINK & ACT LIKE A WINNER

Most people are interested in figuring out a fun, quick, or easy way to be successful, but they're not willing to get into the game or even go to the course. They like to stay back where the water is warm and calm. They think life is easier that way. They get stuck learning from those around them who haven't perfected success. If they continue that trend, most likely they will never figure out that success doesn't come to them in a fun, quick, or easy way.

In fact, success doesn't come to you at all—you go to it! If you want something in life, you have to go and get it!

That's the path that I've followed. That's the path that I inspire others to follow. That's the path that I have seen work.

I want to share with you how successful individuals "get their act together" and what qualities they have developed on their way. Throughout this book, I will provide answers to questions that have been nagging so many people all over the world—questions like, "What are the consistent qualities of high achievers?" "Where did they come from and do I possess them?" and "How can I acquire them?"

Each chapter that follows defines a specific quality you need to think and act like a winner. I provide the necessary strategies for you to develop and implement the behaviors that will bring you to personal and professional greatness. I hope you, too, will enjoy your path to success!

one

Abnormality

*Do you ever consider yourself to be abnormal?
I'm sure we have all, at one time or another, felt
abnormal. Other people have actually told me to my
face that they think I'm abnormal. While most people
would have probably reacted with anger or hurt,
I just smiled and nodded. I took the comment
as a compliment. Why? Good question!*

"Normal" means "average."

"Abnormal," by definition, describes anyone who is exceptional.

It is simply unclear thinking to believe that a normal, or average, person is mentally healthy and an abnormal, or exceptional, person is mentally ill.

If we look at some of the most successful people in history, they were or could have been classified as abnormal. Nobel prize winner Albert Einstein fell short as a student in school, yet today his name is almost synonymous with intelligence and genius. Mahatma Gandhi, who had a hot temper as a child, used nonviolent civil disobedience as a potent form of force in eventually liberating India from British rule.

Jesus Christ was condemned as a criminal because of his teachings, yet today it's estimated that about two billion believers practice those teachings. Inventor Thomas Edison kept looking for success in creating an alkaline battery, and he finally found it after more than eight thousand experiments. Eight thousand! How many normal people would have kept on trying after so many attempts?

Some individuals from more recent times whom I consider to be abnormally successful are Tiger Woods, who at 21 became the youngest golf player to ever win the Masters Tournament and who continues to shatter other records; Bill Gates, a shy college-dropout who became the multibillionaire leader of software giant Microsoft Corporation; and Warren Buffet, who has acquired millions and millions of dollars by following the once nontraditional strategy of investing in undervalued companies whose value rose over time. That strategy is common advice nowadays.

You might be thinking to yourself, "These people aren't abnormal," but by definition, they are! They were or still are better than average.

I don't know about you, but I'd rather be labeled as abnormal, since it suggests that I could be exceptional instead of just average.

What is the difference then between those who are normal and those who are abnormal? Consider the following traits.

Exceptional People . . .	Whereas Average People . . .
Are open to new things and to learning new things.	Resist new ideas, preferring the status quo.
Allow their actions to speak louder than words.	Just talk.
Try to develop themselves in any way they can.	Use only their current skills, believing that these skills will carry them indefinitely.
Are focused, driven, and motivated.	Have scattered and unclear thoughts.
Stand up for what they believe in, such as living and standing by their commitments, values, and morals.	Change their beliefs, ideas, and behaviors to meet the popular majority.
Focus on others and their needs.	Focus on themselves.
Focus on the details, the little things—things that are truly important, like love, kindness, giving, and family.	Obsess over negativity and others' actions.
Accept that they are self-employed (more on this later) and take responsibility for their work and actions; they create their own destiny.	Believe that society owes them and that others will provide for them.
Use and seek out their talents, capitalizing on their human creativity.	Stay stagnate in their thoughts, actions, and beliefs.
Have clear written goals and believe in collaboration and teamwork. They also have a vision for the future.	Believe "whatever will be, will be."
Are unselfish. They give their time, their treasures, and their talents.	Justify why they don't have resources or time.
Realize that goals are dreams with a timeline. They understand that there are no limits to how awesome one can become or how high one can rise, except for the limits that one imposes on oneself.	Blame external circumstances for their failure.

So now, would you rather be considered normal or abnormal . . . average or exceptional?

My challenge for you is to do everything with an abnormal attitude. Break free from being average and become exceptional! Jump from being ordinary to being extraordinary!

Realize, though, that this challenge may not be easy. It depends on what you truly want and how much you truly want it.

If you want to be exceptional, be prepared to offer dedication, focus, and sacrifice. Fight urges to seek out distractions from what you ultimately desire in life. Resist the temptation to be just like everyone else! When faced with choices, remember that abnormal people are willing to do what normal people won't do. This makes all the difference.

Nothing splendid has ever been achieved

except by those who dared believe

that something inside them

was superior to circumstances.

~ Bruce Barton

THINK & ACT LIKE A WINNER

t w o

Comfort Zone

*You have probably heard of the term "comfort zone."
It is often used to describe the habits that we develop
over a period of time.*

Although these habits may initially grow out of our deepest needs, they can eventually harden into a barrier. The barrier tends to prevent us from realizing our greatest potential.

For example, we need to eat. Our bodies require nutrients from the food we eat in order to function. However, for some people, this basic human need can become a problem. Perhaps one overeats when he or she is not even hungry. Perhaps the person becomes obese, endangering his or her health. This barrier of overeating when not hungry can eventually contribute to the person not realizing his or her potential for physical fitness.

If we want to break habits that do not serve us in striving to reach our personal and professional goals, then we must first look at how habits are formed.

A habit becomes part of your comfort zone when you expect to experience it or look forward to experiencing it every day. For example, how many people start their days with a morning cup or more of coffee? How many times does a family head to the ski lodge in Colorado, the theme parks in central Florida, or the beaches in the Caribbean so that they can visit their favorite vacation spot over and over? How many Monday night (or any night) bowling leagues do you think there are? And how about the same stuff/different day at work?

You might be thinking that some of these expectations are positive things. Coffee might make you more alert. Regular family vacations build fond memories. Bowling teams have fun. And work pays the bills, right?

The problem with these expectations is that they could, not definitely will, but very well could, lead to habits that put us in a comfort zone. "Hey," you might say, "Sounds comfortable! What's wrong with having all these enjoyable habits that make me feel comfortable?"

What's wrong is that anything you might want to do that is outside of your comfort zone can threaten your feelings of comfort.

"Try some tea? There's not as much caffeine as in coffee! Go to Las Vegas instead of Florida? But I don't gamble! Stay home with my spouse? But bowling night's my getaway night! Take on a different responsibility at work? But I'm good at what I do now!"

All of these excuses can be valid reasons for not changing one's habits. But . . . if the reason you don't want to change your ways is to avoid the discomfort caused by trying new things, then that's a surefire sign that you've settled into a comfort zone.

If an act seems too uncomfortable to do, then we tend to

view it as a negative activity and provide excuses like the ones mentioned above. When we run from what we view as a negative activity, we cannot move forward, whether in our work, relationships, or lifestyle.

For example, a person who refuses to try tea would miss out on tasting some wonderful contemporary flavors such as black-raspberry or vanilla-maple. A person who avoids Vegas would miss out on all the many shows, sights, and activities that the city offers to non-gamblers. A person who goes bowling to get away from a spouse is probably the person who should be spending time communicating with the spouse— what love is that person missing out on? A person who avoids new challenges at work also avoids new opportunities for more knowledge and skills or raises and advancements.

By not moving forward, we are staring a barrier right between the eyes . . . without even knowing it!

If you are like most individuals, you look forward to certain activities that make you feel comfortable and give you an "at-home" feeling. It is that same "at-home" feeling that can keep you stuck if you don't try new things. To break your comfort zone, you must step back, evaluate, and step up!

Step Back—One morning, decide to stay in bed for about ten minutes before you get out of bed.

Evaluate—Take that time to think about what happens in a typical day for you. Does it too often conform to a familiar pattern? Were you planning to have the same kind of day today?

Step Up—Decide to make a change in your typical day. Not a change just for the sake of change. I've learned that to change is to grow, and to grow is to change! You cannot have one without the other. Stepping up, or inviting change, involves taking risks. They don't have to be huge ones; they can be taken in small steps. The process can be difficult and challenging, and the growth or lesson may not always seem positive, but you learn through the process, and learning fosters personal development.

Recently, I made a much-needed addition to my staff. The additional help has ultimately proven to be of great value to the office. But back when I first made the hire, even though I had been ready for the personnel expansion, some of my staff were overwhelmed by the change. The cause of stress was not due to my hiring someone else to help out but to the change in office routine. The "community comfort zone" was broken. Responsibilities were added, changed, and redirected, adding pressure to the work environment. The pressure led to excuses, demands, and complaints. But we all stepped back, evaluated the situation, and stepped up to the challenges presented by the change.

This example demonstrates how easily a newly introduced element can break the comfort zone. The fact is that change happens naturally every day; it does not have to be introduced (unless we recognize we have fallen into a miserable rut that we want to change).

When you recognize discomfort in yourself due to a change, ask yourself how to respond in such a way that will help the situation. If you learn to adapt and respond to change rather than react to it, you can more easily break your comfort zone.

It's said that insanity involves doing the same thing over and over while expecting a different result each time. Many of us want to make positive changes in our lives, but we continue to act with the same old habits that keep us from stretching into new areas of growth, success, and change. We need to step back, evaluate, and step up, just as Mary Kay Ash did.

In 1963, Ms. Ash had the audacity to think that beauty products would sell at home demonstrations at a time when no one else had ever even conceived of, let alone agreed with, the notion. She believed her skin care products could be sold to small groups of women who were looking for ways to improve their image and potential success. Her first home show produced $1.50 in sales. Mary Kay had risked her entire life savings, $5000, on this venture, so $1.50 in sales was not a good return on her investment. However, she did not pack up and go home to ease her discomfort. Packing up her cosmetics and going to women's homes were still a major part of her business plan, but she modified her selling techniques, refined her packaging, and adjusted her attitude. One year later, she made $34,000 in retail sales. Fifteen years later, Mary Kay Cosmetics had 150,000 independent beauty consultants and 3,000 sales directors producing gross sales of $200 million. As of this writing, there are about 600,000 beauty consultants and sales directors serving customers in 35 countries!

I am always inspired by stories of those who have stretched their comfort zones and entered into places where doubt lies. I encourage you to step back, evaluate, and step up—I invite you to question your habits and break your comfort zone! Learn to force yourself into the unknown. Trying something new may be an uncomfortable task, but if you don't try, you may never know how far you can really go.

Survival

Every morning in Africa, a gazelle wakes up.

It knows it must run faster than the fastest lion

or it will be killed.

Every morning a lion wakes up.

It knows it must outrun the slowest gazelle

or it will starve to death.

It doesn't matter whether you are a lion or a gazelle:

when the sun comes up, you'd better be running!

~ Unknown

THINK & ACT LIKE A WINNER

A year from now,

you may wish you had started today.

~ Karen Lamb

THINK & ACT LIKE A WINNER

three

Charisma

*I think one of the most important qualities a
successful person can have is charisma.
I actually would place it first on a list of
"Qualities of Success" because of the tremendous impact
it has on getting ahead in work and life.*

Y ou don't have to be as funny as a Seinfeld, as suave as a Connery, as sophisticated as a Diana, or even as loud and obnoxious as a Costanza to have charisma. You just have to be positive, fun, confident, and give others the feeling that you and they are alive.

People love charisma! We choose to buy from people who possess charisma, because they're more likeable. We enjoy seeing and spending time with charismatic people because they share laughter and joy with us.

I don't know too many people who want to be around snobs, wimps, meanies, whiners, or know-it-alls. The negativity of these types of people breeds more negativity, just as positive energy attracts positive energy. You can hang around people that make you feel good or make you feel bad, but it's you who must choose which people you want to affect your life.

Do you think you can avoid the negative impact of negative

people? Consider the saying, "You are what you eat." The same concept can hold true for the connection between you and the people you interact with every day. In other words, "You become who you hang around."

Do you know any negative people? Are there any in your family, at the office, or in your neighborhood? They aren't fun to be around, are they?

When we choose to be around negative people, we have to be very careful. If we're not, we could allow them to bring us down. Their negativity can bring out negativity in us and have adverse effects on our attitude, performance, or ethics, which directly impacts our ability to think and act like the winners we are or aim to be.

Could you imagine spending one day with Tiger Woods? Jim Carrey? Zig Ziglar? Can you imagine how different you would feel with them compared to being with the negative people you know?

If you looked around yourself, though, you would see Tigers and Jims and Zigs in your own circle of associates; you simply need to map out which personality characteristics you feel are beneficial to your success and associate with those whom you feel have those characteristics (besides incorporating those characteristics into your own personality, of course). After all, you have the ability to choose which direction you travel.

This doesn't mean you ignore people. Let's face it, if you have a negative boss or co-worker, you may still have to work with them. In this circumstance, you need to make sure that you opt for positive choices when you're around them. You don't have to be negative just because they are! And who knows, perhaps your positive characteristics will rub off on them.

This topic always reminds me of the saying from an old philosopher, "When you are on fire, people will line up to watch you burn!" It's so true! The outgoing, friendly, funny, people who are having a good time are usually the ones who get noticed. People want to be around them and be their friends. People who make no attempt to be interesting or liven things up tend not to get noticed. Does the term "wallflower" mean anything?

I never saw myself as being very popular or charismatic, but over time, as I became more confident in myself, I found that others liked to be with me. I naturally started behaving in a more outgoing manner and eventually started having more fun in my life. Being relaxed and feeling free to let myself shine had a positive impact on me and a positive response from those around me. Exactly how did I manage to develop my charisma? The practices below are ones that I applied and that you too can apply daily to improve your personal charisma.

Like yourself—If you want others to like you, you have to like yourself first. Resolve that you are who you are, a wonderful person with unique gifts and talents to offer, and like yourself unconditionally. Such a disposition builds high self-esteem, which transfers over to others.

Take an interest in how you groom and dress yourself—Part of your charisma depends on your appearance. You feel good about yourself when you look great, and when you look great, you more often than not feel great. Others will see your confidence and react positively to it.

Be good at what you do—Whether you like your job or not, be good at it. This expertise builds an air of confidence. Others will recognize your skills and will compliment you, which not only helps your reputation but also your self-esteem.

Be aware of the silent messages that you send—Gestures, eye contact, body language, touching, and animation are all nonverbal methods of communication. Do you shuffle your feet, or do you stand tall? Do you send messages that drive people away, or do you build a captive audience with your silent messages? Nonverbal communication can mean more than spoken words!

Listen—Take an interest in others. Find out what makes them tick. Ask them questions about themselves, their day, their hobbies, and their jobs. Let your audience, associate, or customer talk, and really listen to what they say so that you can respond appropriately. Good listening skills make you more attractive to others.

Adapt well to others—Determine their type of personality, search out their interests, and then adapt your disposition to bond with them. Mirror their mannerisms. People automatically like those who are like them, so discover through conversation something that you have in common with them, and let it drive your interaction. Don't pretend to have something in common, as most people can see through pretense, but discover a genuine commonality. Discovering similar tastes in music, movies, or hobbies are often great catalysts.

The more you put the above tenets into practice, the more you will see how much you enjoy being with other people and how much they enjoy being with you.

A man can succeed at almost anything

for which he has unlimited enthusiasm.

~ Charles M. Schwab

THINK & ACT LIKE A WINNER

four

Creativity

Creativity has to be one, if not the, most important part of achieving elevated performance. Through my travels, I have met some of the most creative people imaginable. I am not talking about the "artsy type", but rather the visionary type of creators—the problem-solvers whose ideas and suggestions keep you up at night because they have set your mind racing with what is possible.

Highly creative people can't sit still. They work from project to project. They see the unseen. They paint pictures in their mind of what their project will look like when it's done. Interestingly enough, they don't necessarily focus on how to get there. They don't even focus on the details in the middle. What they actually see is how the end will look—they see the destination—then they work backwards to map out the journey from destination to starting point.

Some people start a project with basic information and then define the steps needed to reach completion, without ever understanding what the end result may be until they are close to it. By that point, their linear thinking tends to make them become unclear as to how the project will actually pan out. Some simply give up because of their frustration. Others hope that whatever the result ends up being will suffice. Successful projects cannot proceed in that way. Successful projects require creativity.

Because I've found that top achievers are truly creative, I want to help teach you how to become more creative. The best way I can express what I mean is by having you do an experiment. Put your imagination to work for me for a minute.

Imagine that you are taking a walk through a beautiful forest. Picture the green leaves of the trees and the fresh smell of pine. Try to find a path that you are familiar with, one with lots of scenery that is not too difficult to navigate.

Now, imagine walking with your head down, focusing on your shoes. Don't look up. Instead, focus completely on your feet. Walk as long as you can without looking up. What do you see? Do you see anything besides your feet and the dirt and leaves on your path? No, how could you?

Creative people live with their head up high. They not only look at the path in front of them, but they also look into the trees, seeing the wind blowing through the leaves. They see other paths and directions in which they can travel. They hear the chirping of birds and insects, and the swash of a far-off cascading waterfall. They search out the diversity and beauty around them, and they use what they perceive to their advantage.

Now do the same experiment looking up instead of down. What do you see? You can see what the creative person can see.

Some call this vision. I call it creativity. Many of us have vision, but only a select few can see a situation in five different ways within seconds.

Let me give you an example. A few years ago, I took an assessment of my abilities. The assessment dealt with five different areas of intelligence and then went into personal interests and other major areas. When I was a child, test-taking was one of my greatest fears. I was not very good with grammar, spelling, and math. Timed tests just worsened my performance.

As an adult taking this assessment, I felt my heart pound fast inside my chest, and my hands got sweaty and clammy, just like when I was a kid. As a result, I did not score well in four of the five areas of the assessment. However, I was shocked at my results in the area of problem-solving.

That particular test consisted of solving ten problems in two minutes by mentally taking a shape, turning it over, turning it backward, changing its color, rotating it again, and the like. To my amazement, I scored perfectly on all ten.

The reason I share this story is to prove that even though I failed in the other areas of intelligence, I was able to picture in my mind's eye a changing object and predict its final outcome. Many highly creative people can do this. They picture what the end result is going to be before they act. They may need help with directions along the way, but they know what the result is supposed to look like.

How can you enhance your creativity? Try practicing the exercises below.

Start with the end—In your job, at home, and with your friends, keep the end in mind when you begin a project. For example, picture how the kitchen will look when you are done cleaning it, before you actually begin cleaning it. Another example: Imagine how will you will feel when you're done organizing the garage, before you begin organizing it. Think about where everything will fit and how you can place things to make it more efficient.

See it—Picture the result in your mind's eye. For example, Bill Gates paints a mental picture of where he wants to go, and then he explains it to his employees the way he sees it.

Don't forget the details—Do you remember the memory card-game Concentration that you played growing up, where you turned over two cards at a time to find matches? The same concept applies to nearly any situation, problem, or project. You just have to see the end result and find your way to it by using details as stepping stones. Don't focus too much on the details, but don't forget them either.

Start projects at home that help bring out your creative side—Paint, plant, build, draw, or sew. Do something conceptual that will make you think.

Avoid looking at problems head-on—Start viewing problems from other angles. Highly creative people like to use the phrases "devil's advocate" or "poking holes." They like to see things from all angles so that they are able to find the best way to reach their goal.

Know this: There is nothing more empowering than an idea whose time has come! Be creative, and watch your self-confidence rise!

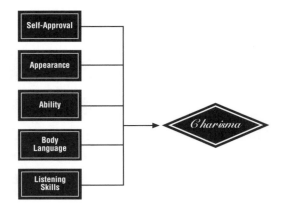

THINK & ACT LIKE A WINNER

Start thinking of yourself as an artist
and your life as a work-in-progress.
Works-in-progress are never perfect,
but changes can be made . . .
Art evolves—So does life.
Art is never stagnant—Neither is life.
The beautiful, authentic life
you are creating for yourself is your art.
It's the highest art.

~ Sarah Ban Breathnach

THINK & ACT LIKE A WINNER

five

Know-How

What is know-how and how is it defined as a characteristic of high performance?

Know-how is the knowledge and skill required to do something correctly.

It also includes characteristics such as intelligence, knowledge, and being teachable, or rather, being willing to learn. The main thrust of this last characteristic is to know that you can be taught and to allow yourself to be open to learning.

Throughout my career, I have come upon many individuals that want to be more successful. They want to make more money and move up in the world. Who doesn't? What amazes me is that when I ask them what they are doing to facilitate their desires, they respond with one of three answers: "Well I'm looking for a new job," "I've taken on a second job," or "Uh, nothing."

Remember the classic saying, "You've gotten what you have by doing what you've always done." If you want something different than what you have now, you have to change what you do in the future. It really is that simple.

Know-how is vital to our growth. It is what makes us more marketable to the public. Think of yourself as a product (because you are). What makes you valuable? Are you better than the other product sitting next to you on the shelf? Would you sell yourself in the finest of retail shops, or do you think that your product would be sold at a discount store? Are you like an SUV, or are you like a little red wagon?

Your knowledge, talents, and skills ultimately determine your worth in the marketplace. The problem is that many of us think we know more than we do.

Many of us believe there are three ways we can be taught: learn from our peers, a master, or ourselves.

Can we teach ourselves? Can we teach ourselves how to be more successful? Can we teach ourselves how to make more money? I say no, not at all. Many would disagree, but think of it this way: If you sat in a box for a month with no exposure to the outside world, could you come out knowing trigonometry? Of course not! You could learn only if you were taught or if you had resources like a textbook. Standard ways of learning are by trial and error, and from exposure to certain situations. We learn from external circumstances, which means that we can't learn completely from ourselves.

Then where do we get the know-how to become more successful? Some learn from the second source, their peers. Unfortunately, many of them don't know any more than what you do.

Think about it. Do we classify ourselves? Can you classify by income level the different parts of your city? Of course you can! East side, west side, south side, the right side of the tracks . . . you get the picture. You can often tell block by block what type of social status the people in your community have. Think of your friends. Do they make about the same amount of money that you do, give or take a few bucks? Do they pretty much do the same things that you do? Do they learn from the same sources that you do? Yes, yes, and yes? Then how much do you think you can really, honestly learn from the people who are in the same circles that you are?

Let me take a different approach to make my point. Have you ever dreamed about how others live, such as celebrities, doctors, or CEOs . . . you know, rich people? Have you ever wondered where they got their money or their social status? What did they do? How did they get there? Where does their money come from? How can they afford that big house? When you go back to your friends and neighbors, you sit around and ask the same questions, and no one has the answers.

The best way for us to learn is from the third option—learn from a master. As my father told me, "If you want to play golf well, hang out at the golf course, not the pool!"

Many work environments have mentor programs. What an excellent way of learning from a master! You choose someone who is at the level of success at which you want to be, and you learn from the mentor how he or she got there. You hang around with that person and you ask questions, make notes, and take direction. Learning from a master takes humility. You must be open to admitting that you don't "know it all." Only then can you move forward, learn more, and become more knowledgeable. In turn, you will become more valuable in the marketplace.

A survey of more than 300 companies nationwide found that companies are focusing on developing the leadership abilities of managers, executives, and employees internally through coaching and mentoring programs:

• 59% currently offer coaching or other developmental counseling to their managers and executives. Another 20% plan to offer coaching within the next year.

• 25% have set up formal mentoring programs, with another 25% planning to do so within the next 12 months.

Coaching and mentoring programs are becoming valuable developmental and retention tools for many organizations.

Reasons for offering mentoring programs:

• Retention of employees — 73%

• Improve leadership and managerial skills — 71%

• Develop new leaders — 66%

• Enhance career development — 62%

• Put high-potential individuals on the fast career track — 49%

• Promote diversity — 48%

• Improve technical knowledge — 30%

The survey was conducted by Manchester, a human capital consulting services subsidiary of Modis Professional Services of Jacksonville, FL, a global provider of business services including consulting, outsourcing, training, and strategic staffing services on March 2, 1999.

This concept is true in your personal life as well. Suppose you want a fulfilling marriage. If your parents always fought and ended up not speaking to each other for days, would you ask them the secrets to what makes a successful marriage? Or would you ask your Aunt Ann and Uncle Bill, who always discussed their disagreements, worked out their conflicts, and have been happily married for 40 years?

THINK & ACT LIKE A WINNER

When you go to those in the know, you can know too!

Following are some ways in which you can increase your know-how.

Find someone who has already successfully done what you want to accomplish, and stick by them—Don't leave! Breathe in every piece of information you can. Take notes. Do whatever your chosen expert suggests and follow the same pattern he or she did. Be committed to what it takes, even if it involves starting over or going in a completely different direction, which is when most people stop. They don't want to change or give up what they have come to expect (they don't want to break out of their comfort zones), so they never achieve their dreams. Don't let fear and lack of humility deter you. Remember that if someone else, the master, has done it, you can too!

Accept that what you know isn't enough—This is not to say that your current know-how won't serve you. It will for what you currently do. But if you want more out of life, don't get caught in the trap of thinking that you know all there is to know about a subject. There is always something more to learn! In fact, the more you learn, the more you will see there is to learn. Become a sponge for knowledge and continue to absorb more and more. Keep learning a life-long proposition.

Read—Readers are leaders! If you read one book a month, you will learn enough to accomplish the equivalent of a college degree in less than five years. Magazines, the Internet, and community newspapers all have information that will enhance your know-how, if you discern which ones to look at and which to ignore.

Listen to vocabulary tapes—Vocabulary determines intelligence to those who don't know you. It impresses upon those you meet that you have know-how. Studies have proven that the number one common characteristic of top CEOs is not wealth, education, family ties, a Harvard or Yale education . . . it's not drive, dedication, or having vision . . . All of these things are great and have certainly helped these people achieve their goals, but the number one characteristic that aids these businesspeople is their vocabulary. Vocabulary helps you lead people where they want to be led. Reading with a dictionary at your side is another way to improve your vocabulary.

Assess the knowledge and skills that you currently have—What are they worth to the market? How can you sell them to the people who can help you advance? Would those people buy them? Why or why not? You need to ask yourself these questions and write down the answers before you can go out to gain more money and success or meet your goals. If you don't assess what your know-how is, how can you enhance it? Do it now! Don't delay.

Make a list of the knowledge and skills you need to arrive at your desired destination—Once you've assessed your current know-how, determine what knowledge you need. Research and find out what resources will help you attain the knowledge and skills you desire, then get them! Again, don't delay! In this era of information, research data can change overnight.

Know that if you're not getting better, you're getting worse—If you're getting worse, then your competition can surpass what you have accomplished so far. To stay ahead, you must commit to continuous learning.

We can get over being poor,

but it takes longer to get over being ignorant.

~ Jane Sequichie Hifler

THINK & ACT LIKE A WINNER

six

Dream Your Success

Dreamers are always looking for something bigger and better. They are searchers, never satisfied with the mundane, always striving for more with restlessness and hunger. Every time I hear the song "Hungry Heart" by Bruce Springsteen, I think of a dreamer, a searcher. He sings, "Everybody has a hungry heart, lay down your money and play your part—because everybody has a hungry heart."

Searchers have hungry hearts. They are constantly hunting for greater things. One of the distinct elements of a searcher is that he or she is never content with the way things are. To dreamers, anything and everything have room for improvement.

Searchers are also risk takers. They are willing to take on the most difficult of challenges in order to reap the bountiful rewards that follow. As author Frederick Wilcox said, "Progress always involves risk; you can't steal second base and keep your foot on first."

Do you search for or dream of success?

What is success to you?

Defining success is difficult because it is different for each individual. Having your own business, owning a six-bedroom home with an indoor heated pool and five fireplaces, driving a Mercedes-Benz, sending your children to a good college, keeping family relations intact, or marrying a beauty queen or rock star are all examples of what defines success to different people.

Whatever success means to you, I have found certain elements to be common in a great number of high performers. My many years of speaking and training have brought me to realize that if you want to be successful, or a high performer, you would do well to consider the following suggestions.

Successful people seek out other successful people—Find a mentor. Call and invite him or her to lunch. Ask your mentor questions. Follow his or her advice. Also consider that a time will come when you outgrow your mentor, so be open to searching for mentors that continuously augment your personal success.

Successful people develop a healthy balance between their personal and professional lives—They take the time to plan their day and map out short-term and long-term goals. They set limits inside as well as outside of the work environment. For example, when I am at work, I focus on the projects I'm working on. When I come home to my wife and children, I don't discuss work. I leave my work matters at the office and my family matters at home.

Successful people learn what drives themselves and others— Simply put, they listen. They pay attention to themselves, their surroundings, and the people they interact with, and then they use what they perceive to act in such a way that ensures the most positive environment possible. They also initiate enthusiasm and motivation.

Successful people set goals and limits—They know when and how to say yes or no. They realize how to create harmony instead of stress when it arises in their sphere.

Ask yourself what success feels like. What do you need to do to achieve it? If you dream your success and then search it out, you are bound to find it.

I always knew I would do something,

and do it right. I believed it.

I mean, I really, really believed it.

I think you have to

if you're going to make it happen.

~ Tommy Hilfiger

Attitudes are contagious.

Do you want people around you to catch yours?

~ *Bob Moawad*

THINK & ACT LIKE A WINNER

seven

Instinct,
Intelligence & Intuition

When speaking of their pets, people often refer to their animal's instinct. What is instinct? What makes an animal know when a food is safe to eat or a place is safe to roam?

Instinct is a powerful innate motivation, impulse, capability, or aptitude. The key thing about instinct is that it is impelled from within.

How good are your instincts? Are you the type to "go for it" or "play it safe?" Do you ever have the feeling that you should do something, but then you end up talking yourself out of it?

Why do we have instincts and why do they have such power over us?

Instinct comes from within. Some people have better instincts than others, and I believe it is because they are more in tune with their environment.

Daily, we consume data from external forces, sometimes without even realizing it. A song on the radio could make us reminiscent; content from a television show could make us laugh or cry; another person's enthusiasm could lift or disengage us; the weather could induce depression or cheer. How does your environment affect you?

Our brains take in information from our environment, circumstances, and realities, and then it categorizes that information into different areas in our subconscious. When we have a need for it, we access the information, although we generally don't remember the root of its origin. Often without our conscious awareness, our belief system and intelligence are affected by what we have ingested from our environment.

There are three types of intelligence: analytical, creative, and practical. Those who have good instincts are more geared toward practical intelligence. They don't evaluate why things happen but just accept that gut feelings are viable solutions to most any situation. They use what they know instinctively, yet practically, to conduct their activities. They tend to think practically, not analytically. Consider the following example of practical intelligence.

John considers himself the smartest in his class. He likes to make fun of Scott, the boy he has identified as dumbest in the class. John pulls aside his friend Tom and says, "You want to see what 'stupid' means, Tom? Watch this . . . 'Hey, Scott, here are two coins. Take whichever one you want. It's yours.'"

Scott looks at the two coins, a nickel and a dime, for a moment, and then selects a nickel. "Go ahead, Scott, take it, it's yours," John laughs. Scott takes the larger coin and walks away.

An adult who has been watching the transaction from a distance walks up to Scott and points out that the dime is worth more than the nickel, even though it is smaller, and that Scott has just lost five cents.

"Oh, I know that," replies Scott, "but if I had picked the dime, John would never ask me to choose between the two coins again. I've already collected over a dollar from him, and all I have to do is keep choosing the nickel."

Some students can be slow to learn in school or they might have a hard time taking tests while at the same time being able to think clearly "outside the box" in any situation. This person could very well be the one who sees every setback as an opportunity and does a 360-degree review of any situation quickly and easily.

The same can be said of highly intelligent people: Some who understand the highest academic concepts might have no basic or common sense whatsoever.

The person who can memorize facts without being able to apply them practically and the person who can get things done without understanding the theory behind what they've done are the ones who represent the distinction between "book-smart" and "street-smart." Often, the street-smart person has stronger instincts.

One of the best examples of this type of instinct and common sense can be found in my good friend, Patrick Combs. Patrick is a successful author and speaker. Like me, he started out in the public speaking business at a very young age. We both approached our careers from different angles. I did it the hard way! In the beginning of my career, I thought linearly instead of laterally. Quite frankly, *I only knew what I knew!*

But Patrick, who is not your typical, average person, has an amazing way of thinking of things in a unique and different way, using a combination of common sense and instinct. He thought "out of the box." He didn't want to keep running engagement to engagement, concentrating on booking as many clients as possible. He wanted to launch himself as fast as possible. So, he went straight to the top and focused on one single customer, and he hit it big.

Patrick finished writing his book, *Major In Success*, for the college-student market. But he had a dilemma. How many college students would have money to hire Patrick to speak on their campuses? He'd be lucky if they had ten dollars for his book! Most colleges have speakers, but they don't have a big budget for speaking engagements. Patrick could have worked very hard writing, sending letters, calling people, and taking any speaking engagement he could get, but that wasn't good enough. He wanted faster, easier success.

So he went to the people who have the money. He did what I call **ASE**. He **Analyzed** the situation, developed **Strategies** to beat the system, and then he **Executed** his plan.

Patrick knew from his college experience that Visa and MasterCard set up booths in the campus cafeterias every month, giving out candy, pens, and other items in order to entice students to sign up for a credit card. Because of his lateral thinking, Patrick now had the perfect clients to pitch to; if he could get Visa or MasterCard to pay for his speaking, he would have it made.

But why would one of the largest Fortune 500 companies in the nation want to pay Patrick to speak at colleges?

He knew that colleges were a little tired of Visa and MasterCard coming back every month. The way he saw it, if the companies sponsored Patrick's presentations for a goodwill tour, they could offer something of more value than candy or pens. A college would welcome a motivational speaker more than they would a booth pushing credit cards. So he added a section to his book about the importance of establishing credit during one's college years, then he began calling, writing, and talking to whomever he could in order to secure a meeting to pitch his idea.

Finally he received an appointment with the marketing director for Visa. He knew this was a great opportunity, so he prepared well. Prior to the appointment, he told himself

THINK & ACT LIKE A WINNER

over and over to keep calm, play it cool, and try to win over Visa. He needed to sell them on why he was the best and how he could give them a winning show. He needed to assure them that he'd have wonderful materials to present. He needed to explain how his audience would respond enthusiastically to his presentations. More importantly, he'd have to explain how Visa could benefit from this alliance. All of this was what Patrick had in mind when he walked into the Visa office that day.

But following is what actually happened.

Patrick was nervous, but his instinct set in just before he entered the marketing director's office. He threw out his prepared notes and rehearsed presentation, and he started by announcing, "Let's face it, your reputation on college campuses is shot! Activity directors accuse you of getting students in debt, and they're banning you from tabling on their campuses."

"I have a solution for you. Sponsor me to do success seminars at college campuses all across the nation. We won't push credit cards, we'll promote the responsible use of credit cards, and of course, success. Colleges trust me so they'll welcome the tour – you'll benefit from my reputation. As the sponsor, you'd pick up the tab for each speech, and in return your logo will be included on banners and posters – we'll call it the 'Visa Success Tour.' I'll get you back into good standing with colleges, and I'll successfully promote your brand at the same time."

How do you think he was doing so far?

Just wait . . . there's more!

Patrick's negotiation skills started to stir. He continued,

"In order to do this, you will need to invest a small amount of money. I'll need $500,000 for travel, promotions, and the ability to hire a staff member."

Do you think his execution of this strategy worked? It did!

What powerful negotiation skills Patrick possesses! He taught me that people love to buy things that appear to be first class. If it is too cheap, they will wonder if what they are buying is not the best. So you can presume that the higher your price, the more in demand you will be.

Patrick followed his instinct, and it paid off. Not only did Visa like his style, they agreed with him that they needed a better relationship with the college market. They not only hired him for the job, but they added *one million dollars* to his proposal. They also signed Patrick for two years instead of one.

Patrick's common sense approach and instinct to think "out of the box" paid off in a big way, launching his career to a new level. The tour took him to the 100 biggest universities in the country.

Intuition, or insight on a subconscious level, is closely related to instinct. How do we learn to act on our instincts? Through intuition. I believe that intuition is a capacity you're born with, like language or the appreciation of music. Intuition is not a power that you can acquire, but luckily, you already have it! It's an integral part of everyone's mental, emotional, and physical processes. Once you begin to be more aware of your intuition, you can act on it in ways that move you toward success in all areas of your life.

Focus on becoming more aware of yourself and your surroundings. Bring what you pick up on a subconscious level to a conscious level. When you become more aware, you can act on what you perceive and make it an effective tool in your everyday lifestyle.

Every minute of the day, we receive information intuitively, although we are most often unaware of this process occurring. Your intuition is used in the practical decisions made daily, from choices as mundane as what to eat for dinner, what time to go to bed, or what projects to start at work first. The trick to using intuition more effectively is to bring the unconscious data it supplies to a place where the conscious mind can interpret and use it. It takes work and guidance to put this process into practice and eventually learn how to control it.

You need the ability to develop information that you already possess. Instinct and intuition are with us at all times; developing them is a question of how, or if, we access them. For example, not too long ago, I went shopping for a red Jeep. I like the style of Jeeps, and I wanted to see if one would fit my needs. So my wife and I drove to the Jeep dealership. I looked but waited to buy. For the next week, whenever I was on the road, red Jeeps seemed to be everywhere! In fact, it was as if red Jeeps were practically all I saw driving on the streets. Why was that so? Was it because there really were more red Jeeps on the road, or was it that I became more consciously aware of red Jeeps? The latter, absolutely! I had moved the idea of buying a red Jeep from an unconscious desire to a reality pictured at the front of my brain.

When we can move inner insight to the fore, we can more effectively apply our instinct and intuition.

Here's another example. In my office, a client and I conversed about a project we were working on. All of a

sudden, she stopped and shouted out, "Mark Delaney!"
"Who is Mark Delaney?" I responded.

She said, "My husband and I were talking about this fellow
we know and neither of us could remember his name. It has
been bugging me for three days. It just now popped into my
head." "Why did you just come up with this now?" I asked
her. "I don't know. I just did!" she replied.

Have you ever experienced this? When you are trying to
think of something specific (such as somebody's name), it's
sometimes hard to come up with the information that you
need. You'll find that when you stop thinking about it, the
information will come to you unexpectedly. It was there all
the time, you just needed to access it. It takes practice!

To build your instinct and intuition, undertake the
following.

Listen to yourself—Your mind is more powerful than you
think. Intuition exists for a reason; listen to it. Avoid
"beating a situation to death" with negative thinking, and
learn to use positive self-talk to your advantage in working
through your problems. Your instinct will pick up on more
positive things.

Control what goes into your brain—Your instincts derive
from inner knowledge and experience. If you don't fill your
brain with positive, useful information, you may be missing
opportunities that could bring you more success.

Risk it! Don't be afraid to fail—There's a reason that you
feel the way you do, or your instincts wouldn't be telling you
so. Don't let fear deter you from making the choices that are
right for you. Hiding behind your fears may lead you down a
safe path, but perhaps that is not the direction in which you

ultimately want or need to go. Trust and follow your instincts. They are there to protect you.

Don't overanalyze your emotions—Intuition is your brain answering questions for you. The answers will come quickly if you relax your mind, listen to your heart, and avoid picking apart what insights come to you.

Be observant—You may not always realize it, but in trying to evaluate a situation, you could simply be resorting to a pattern that you picked up in the past. Don't allow yourself to get sucked into past patterns. You don't want to numb yourself to presently available elements that are outside of the realm of your past understanding and that could provide you with valuable data for interpretation. Keep your eyes open and allow your brain to take in everything that is present.

Tune into your feelings—Try to identify your feelings by naming them (happy, sad, angry, frustrated, disappointed, excited, and the like). Once you understand how you feel, you will better understand what your instincts are telling you and will be able to act on them appropriately.

Learn to relax—Quiet your mind, especially when you feel confused or uncertain. When you feel these things, sometimes just acknowledging how you feel is enough to quiet your mind. One technique to relax is to breathe deeply (so your abdomen rises and falls) and slowly. When you are relaxed, you can begin to identify what your intuition is presenting to you.

Knowledge has three degrees—

opinion, science, and illumination.

The means or instrument of the first is sense;

of the second, dialectic;

of the third, intuition.

This last is absolute knowledge

founded on the identity of the mind knowing

with the object known.

~ Plotinus

The single greatest talent and tool

that I have tried to master,

that has led me down the road of success . . .

can be found in my ability to paint pictures . . .

compelling vistas that draw others

into the potential of what might be.

~ Bill Gates

THINK & ACT LIKE A WINNER

eight

Map
It Out

*It has always baffled me why we spend so much time
planning our vacations and our weekends,
but when it comes to our everyday lives,
we just "wing it."*

Could you imagine having two weeks off in the summer, driving across the United States, and not bringing a map? Even those individuals who have an excellent sense of direction would need to stop and ask for directions at some point.

The sad part is that when it comes to our personal and professional goals, most of us don't have any sense of direction at all. We just take things as they happen day in and day out. I think the phrase, "I wish I would have done things differently," was created out of this apathetic mindset.

Why is it that many of us have lost our direction? I believe it's because we might not have sat down and drawn out a map of where we're going or where we'd like to go. Sometimes we might even know what we want and how to get there, but we still fall short of our goals. We may get sidetracked or "blow a tire" along the way.

But even then, there's always a spare somewhere—we just need to take the time and initiative to seek it out.

When you visualize where you want to go and put it down on paper, you create your map. It's a simple process. Then you need only to follow the direction in which you want to travel and do what it takes to arrive at your destination!

Here are some tips to keep you focused on the right road.

Create a mission statement—Make it short and simple, and write it down. Read it often to remind yourself of your mission and where you are heading. The statement may change from time to time, or you may have several missions in different areas. Focus always with the end in mind.

Write down your goals, both short-term and long-term— Don't be afraid to dream big! Devise a map/plan that gets you where you want to go. Post these goals everywhere—on your mirror where you'll see them in the morning, in your car, on your desk or computer, on the refrigerator, or any place where it will serve as a boost to you to stay on track with your map. Recognize those skills needed to achieve your goals, and put a deadline on when you will have them mastered. Remember that dreams are goals with deadlines!

Make a list of all the people who are currently doing what you want to do—Repeatedly ask yourself what they did to get there and find the answers. If they are available, ask them questions. Follow their path or adapt the activities to your own style and needs.

Determine what things, if any, you hate to do the most; then do them first—Remember, successful people do what others won't do!

When you have a plan, you feel its pull. Map out your plan and let it fill you with enthusiasm and a burning desire to follow it.

   THINK & ACT LIKE A WINNER

It takes twenty years to

make an overnight success.

~ Eddie Cantor

THINK & ACT LIKE A WINNER

nine

Purpose & Direction

Have you ever run across people who seem to wander aimlessly? They are almost in a type of robot mode, systematically going through each day with no passion or desire for life. I am sure you have; I know I have! They often say things like, "I take what life gives me", or "I roll with the punches".

Isee people like this every day from my office in a busy mall. The expression on their faces never changes. Day after day, they come to work at the mall with the same blank look. In essence, they are living to work rather then working to live. Sadly, these people seem to have no purpose or direction in their lives.

Why am I painting this gloomy picture when I am supposed to be motivating you? Because I want to make sure you are not one of those people, and if you are, I want you to change that today!

What is your purpose? It essentially is your ultimate goal or goals in life. Your purpose is what you envision when you imagine what your life will be like tomorrow, next year, or three years from now. It is what will make you feel happy and satisfied. Without it, you simply go through the motions of life with no passion or desire.

What is direction? It is simply the path that you set to achieve your purpose.

If you already have a sense of purpose and direction, then you have won half the battle in achieving a successful and enriching life.

However, if you think you might be like the wanderers mentioned earlier, those with no sense of purpose or direction, then you have a little more effort to put forth—but it is not too late, I promise! You can change, and you can change right now. All you have to do is close your eyes and think to yourself, "What will really make me happy? In ten years, what do I want to look back on and remember with joy?"

Is achieving a certain title in your career, building a dream house, providing a loving home for your kids, or getting a new education what you long for? Maybe you want to find a loving partner and start a life together. The possibilities are endless—but the solution depends on you. You need to decide what you really want!

As a professional motivational speaker, I am often asked, "Who motivates you?" Because I've been asked this same question many times, I've had a lot of opportunities to rethink my answer. But my response has always pretty much been the same: the positive impact on helping others achieve greatness is what motivates me. I receive many positive rewards from helping people develop and lead successful lives. I know, not think, but know, this is my purpose.

Because I blueprinted my journey by having a purpose and direction, I am successful, happy, and love my work. I am driven by the direction in which my life is headed. I am building an organization through helping others. It's very easy to derive motivation from that alone.

Recently I read an article about a couple that saved relentlessly for fifteen years. They sacrificed anything that was not a necessity for the sake of fulfilling their dream. They planned to have enough money to retire at 40. Their dream was to buy a motor home and spend the rest of their lives traveling the country. Now 42, the couple has been crossing the nation for the past two years. Their story is living proof that dreams really do come true!

Isn't that great? This couple has the freedom to do whatever they want without having to worry about the day-to-day grind. But fulfilling their dream took self-discipline. They had a purpose and a direction while working towards their dream. They blueprinted their journey and achieved their goals: the adventures of traveling and the peace of being financially free.

What are your goals and dreams? Have you found more than one purpose in your life? Do you want to play a more active role in your romantic relationship, in your kids' or grandkids' lives, and in your community?

Part of your success will come from knowing your purpose and heading in the direction toward fulfilling it. What drives you? If you can answer that, you can determine your purpose. If you know your purpose, you can determine your direction.

Most of us have had a sense of purpose and direction at some point in our lives, but perhaps we got lost along the way or we forgot about pursuing what we wanted due to distractions. Maybe we got caught up in other people's ideas of what success is or should be. The amount of money you earn or the level of advancement you achieve in a job will leave you empty and unhappy if it is not in line with your true purpose. Your true purpose will leave you feeling fulfilled and happy. Only you can determine what that is.

I am about to ask you to practice some exercises that will help you determine your purpose and direction. First, remember that life is not about the material things you acquire. You can't take anything with you when it's your time to leave. On your deathbed, do you want to be wishing that you hadn't spent all those late nights at the office? Or will you be proud of your success in all aspects of your life?

What I want to ask you to do is blueprint your journey to success. The key to finding your purpose is to make choices that allow you to enjoy life's small yet valuable treasures. Most people haven't experienced life's potential because they don't know what they want or where they're going. "I just want to live day by day and see what happens" is a common approach people take to life. But if you want to live each day to the fullest, use the steps below to help you determine your purpose, and get on the road to success!

Write your obituary—Use the space that follows to write it, right now. Don't wait! By looking back, you can plan for the future. What do you want it to say? How will others remember you? Were you the angry worker who passed by others' offices each day without even saying a simple, "Hello"? Were you the boss who led the team by setting successful examples? I encourage you to write your obituary based on your life as it is now. This action will help you identify the parts of your life you want to change. Next write an obituary based on how you want your obituary to read. Then live it!

Create a mission statement—Write it down and keep it with you. When people ask you what you do, tell them your mission. For example, when people ask me what I do, my response is quick and sharp, "I make people great!" Their reactions are usually followed by the question, "How do you do that?" I respond by telling them I created this as my mission statement and I focus daily on accomplishing it through my thoughts, words, and actions.

Get involved—This entails more than being involved in your company or work. Getting involved takes moving outside of your comfort zone. Do something that gives back to others, to society, or to your community. Donating money to charities is great, but don't let that be an excuse not to get involved in other ways. If you don't have the money to donate, or if you feel you've already donated enough, there are equally beneficial opportunities for you to get involved. In fact, giving what feels like it would hurt you the most can truly make a difference . . . your time and talent! Applying your time and skills for the benefit of others can turn out to be one of the most rewarding things you'll ever do. Don't let your work success or drive remove you from making mental, physical, and spiritual contributions to making our society greater!

Do what you love, now—I can't stress this enough. Remember the classic saying, "The past is history, the future a mystery, and today is a gift . . . that's why we call it the present." You are given a gift each day—time. I encourage you to spend it wisely. If you ever look back on a day and feel it was wasted, guess what? You have time to make up for it the next day.

Don't be a spectator in your life—Become an active participant! Remember, purpose and direction don't just happen; you have to make them happen.

Perform the steps above now! Waiting will only put you one more day behind in achieving your purpose.

THINK & ACT LIKE A WINNER

Cherish your visions and your dreams

as they are the children of your soul;

the blueprints of your ultimate achievements.

~ Napoleon Hill

THINK & ACT LIKE A WINNER

ten

Vision

The fact that you are reading this book proves that you are interested in achieving a higher level of success. You want to fulfill your desires. You want to enjoy a fine standard of living. You want this life to deliver to you all the good things that you deserve. Being interested in success is a wonderful quality.

The fact that you are reading this book also shows that you have another admirable quality. You have the intelligence to look for tools that will help you get to where you want to go. No matter what you want to build—be it wealth, buildings, or families—going it alone is difficult if not impossible. Many people, in their attempt to build a successful life, forget that there are tools readily available to assist them.

One of the greatest tools ever given to each one of us is that of vision. Vision doesn't cost anything! It is free and unlimited. Successful people train themselves to see not just what is, but what can be. That is vision!

Like many people, I am a dreamer. I have dreams of what I want to accomplish with my time on this earth. I dream of big things, never looking at the safe, secure path. This quality, however, gives some people around me tension.

Indeed, the future can be risky. But to attain great success, you have to envision what can be and take the necessary risks to get there.

Early in my career as a professional speaker, I was feverishly trying to build my base of customers and expose my services to the public in order to make a name for myself. I was having little luck landing the big companies. So, watching what general stores do when they aren't moving merchandise, I had a sale.

For a speaker to hold a sale is difficult because speaking is a service that isn't in high demand from the general public. But I was thinking big. I thought that if I were to reach as many people as possible, I would gain the exposure needed to eventually put me closer to the bigger companies.

I decided to do a free seminar for the public. I had done these in the past and had marginal success, occasionally picking up a customer here or there and always just breaking even. I decided that this time, I would do it bigger than before. I included direct mail, newspaper ads, faxes, telemarketing, and other such promotional techniques. I rented a hotel room, hired a part-time staffer to register attendees, decorated the room, and advertised that I would give away my audiocassette and workbook for free! I believed that last touch would surely bring the people in!

I did a 55,000-piece mail-drop, advertising my free seminar on business success. "Think and Act Like a Winner" was the title. I thought that there must be business owners out there who have employees that lack motivation and drive, and because my seminar was free, that I would have at least 100 people show up. I was getting excited as the weeks drew near to the seminar.

THINK & ACT LIKE A WINNER

After all these preparations were made, I sat down and calculated my total investment. I was happy with what I had accomplished with the budget I was working with—over $4,000 to host the free event. I was pleased!

The day of the event was drawing near and I had very few registration responses. I started to become a little nervous, but because I am a positive thinker, I didn't let it bother me much. My wife and staff, however, were a little more skeptical.

Three days before the event, we had only 15 people registered. That worked out to a cost of $266.66 per person. My mind began to ramble as I calculated the figure. Could I be friendly to these people as they walked in, knowing that it cost me $266.66 just to have them there? How much exposure would I get out of 15 people?

Needless to say, I was starting to get a little more than nervous. I really started worrying! Maybe I wasn't a good speaker. Perhaps I chose a poor topic. Was I a bad marketer? A horrible sales rep? Why is the event going to be such a financial and emotional disappointment? Suppose it happens again the next time I do a seminar. Will I ever be able to make enough money doing what I love?

"WOAH!" I said to myself. "STOP!" Negative thinking would only bring me failure for sure, and thinking about a poor vision of the future would surely attract it.

Zig Ziglar—the world-renowned author, speaker, and change agent—once told me that in the beginning of his career he spoke to everyone possible, anyone who would listen to him. He spent days on the road going from company to company, speaking for whatever they were willing to pay. Now look at him—he is at the top of his field.

I realized that I had to be willing to do what Mr. Ziglar did. If I let the pressures of wanting comfort, a stable job, or a weekly paycheck get to me, then I would quit trying and ruin all chances of living my dream. I'd have to keep my mind on my vision of the future and, like Zig, keep pushing regardless of the outcome. I became determined that the questions darkening my mindset would not distract me.

The day of the event came and we had a grand total of 33 people. I was grateful to those who came. I could have put on a poor performance as a result of the turnout, but I didn't want to disappoint those who had taken the time to come. It was more of a mental drain to do that presentation than any other I'd ever done.

But it paid off. Even though the room was almost empty and the crowd was so small, I visualized that I was coming out on stage in front of 10,000 people. The seminar turned out to be one of my best!

When it was over, I asked all attendees to recommend me to their companies, and I told them that I or one of my staff members would contact them in the near future.

I felt pretty good considering all the circumstances.

The next week, many of my bills came due. My wife and I sat in our office writing checks for each one. As she signed each check she wrote, I heard my wife say over and over, "Wow, that was an expensive lesson." I wanted to agree, but I had to keep my vision.

In an effort to do just that, I started to follow up with those who had attended my seminar. And call after call, I received excuses as to why a company couldn't, wouldn't, or didn't hire speakers or trainers.

Out of the 33 people who attended what I also began to think more and more of as "my expensive lesson," only one actually referred my name to someone in their company who might need my services.

I couldn't hide it any longer—I felt defeated. I knew that, all things considered, $4000 wasn't a lot of money. But that year I had spent many more thousands trying to make it as a speaker, and "my expensive lesson" was almost a final financial blow.

To some people, "my expensive lesson" might have been a sign that perhaps I wasn't meant to be in the business.

But I had a vision of my future.

If I would have given up at that point, you would not be reading this book right now, and I would not have continued to do what I love.

Even though I felt defeated after the free event, I kept on doing what I was doing, kept visualizing where I wanted to be, and kept inching forward. Every day I looked at my computer-screen wallpaper showing a picture of Peter Lowe, motivational maven, on a stage in front of 10,000 people who want to be better than they were yesterday. I didn't give it up; I lived it up—through my vision of what could be.

I have come to believe now that success happens only when one does have a vision of what can be.

Less than eight months after doing that freebie seminar, I received a call from one of the attendees. At the time of the seminar, she was working for a tax, accounting, and business-consulting firm. When I had called on her there, she said the company didn't have a need for my seminars or me. However, she had recently moved to a small town in Iowa and was now working for a co-op. She called and told me that the co-op was having its annual company meeting and she wondered if I would be interested in speaking at the event. I said I would be happy to and planned to discuss details with her and the co-op president the next day.

Originally I thought the annual meeting would be a small get-together of farm co-op members, with a keynote address by me. But after the appointment, I discovered that they were looking for something fun and exciting for over 270 employees, an all-day event that demanded more than just a keynote speech.

I went back to my office to put together a proposal. I thought to myself, "What do I have to lose? Let's do this thing first class!" I made that proposal not just sing but also dance— power-packed prose, full-color graphics, the works!

I sent the proposal back to the board and in less than one day they called me. They loved my ideas and wanted to move forward. They booked me on the spot for over $18,000!

After a bunch of high-fives with my staff, I thought . . . this gig came about as a result of "my expensive lesson."

Of course, now I like to call it "my valuable lesson" instead.

With a vision of what my future could be, I was able to get the deal with the co-op. The great thing is, I am still receiving calls as a result of that free seminar that could have been a career-buster had I not maintained my vision. I have calculated that, as of this writing, I have acquired over $25,000 in revenue because of that "defeat."

How much is a customer worth? You can never know for certain. But you do have to have the vision and stamina to pick up and use the tools for success that are available to you.

THINK & ACT LIKE A WINNER

Nothing in this world is so powerful

as an idea whose time has come.

~ *Victor Hugo*

THINK & ACT LIKE A WINNER

eleven

Initiative

Initiative is a key quality to many employers.
Individuals who show initiative desire and
strive for bigger and better results.
Companies tend to reward these employees
because they have the greatest impact
on the company's ability to grow and succeed.
They are the leaders—the backbone, so to speak.

Initiative is something we all must take accountability and responsibility for on an individual basis. We alone decide when, where, and how much initiative we're going to give on any given project. Anyone can have an idea, but initiative gets the idea expressed and put into action.

Why don't more people take initiative? I believe that fear is the greatest factor. Fear, perhaps of appearing unknowledgeable or looking like a kiss-up, often holds people back and makes them shy away from giving suggestions and sharing ideas.

But if we look at the advantages of taking initiative, we can conquer some of those fears that limit our potential. Know that taking initiative can change your life—at work, at home, anywhere!

One advantage of taking initiative is that it fosters continuous learning, which leads to growth. For example, suppose you are a salesperson who knows your product inside and out. You might also be confident, wise, and look like a million bucks, but if you don't take the initiative to learn about your potential clients before calling upon them, how far do you think you would get? Not very far! A highly successful salesperson knows that learning about each potential customer is key to outsmarting the competition and also to turning the potential customer into an actual customer—due to taking the time to learn about and understand his or her needs. Gaining customers in this fashion leads to growth as a salesperson.

Another advantage of taking initiative is that it makes you more visible to those who can help you succeed. Let's take a look at Joe and Jill, for example. Suppose Joe and Jill both have work hours from 8:00 AM to 5:00 PM, Monday through Friday. Jill comes in every morning at 7:30 AM, gets a cup of coffee, turns on her computer, and plans her day. She's not "on the clock" until 8:00 AM, but she's there every day at 7:30 AM regardless. Joe comes in every day at 7:55 AM. He spends 15 minutes getting ready to start his work day. Who do you think is showing more initiative? Who do you think is going to get recognized by her boss and peers as a leader? When review time comes, you can bet that Jill is going to get a nice raise and possibly a consideration for advancement over Joe.

A third advantage of taking initiative is that it takes you out of your comfort zone. We talked earlier in this book about how do to just that—step back, evaluate, and step up. Remember that doing so leads to personal and professional growth.

Taking initiative also involves a different way of thinking. It helps you to think "out of the box" or be "big-picture oriented." By thinking in this manner, you are more easily able to identify unique and innovative ideas and solutions. You become more creative and active in your relationships with a boss, peer, or spouse. You tend to learn from mistakes, stand up for principles, and challenge current conditions in an effort to improve them.

According to Bob Nelson in his book 1001 Ways to Take Initiative at Work, innovation is the spark that keeps organizations moving ever onward and upward. We innovate to:

1. improve products and services,

2. find a new way to do something,

3. make a task easier or faster,

4. save money,

5. enhance our jobs, and

6. increase our promotability.

New products, new services and new ways of doing business would never come about without innovation. We would be stuck doing the same old things the same old way.

Most organization's problems can be solved routinely 98% of the time. The remaining 2%, usually problems having the greatest effect on the organization, require employee innovation to surpass.

Following are some practices designed to help you increase your ability to take initiative.

Spend 15 minutes every morning planning your day—It might seem that making a daily plan takes up time, but this exercise actually frees up more of your time. When you write a daily plan, the benefits are instantaneous. You get your priorities straight, you waste less time between projects, you stay focused on your goals by being visually reminded of your progress each day, and you meet deadlines. By checking off tasks from your daily plan once they are completed, you gain a greater sense of accomplishment, which builds your confidence and self-esteem. Combine that with having your time and efforts under your control, and you are freed up to initiate more meaningful propositions.

Take risks—Practice going above and beyond expectations. If you do only what is required of you, you're limiting your opportunities for learning and growth. If you do more than what is required, you learn, grow, and get noticed by those in a position to help you on your path.

Be persistent—See projects through to completion. What you think is the end might actually be a stepping stone. Remember Edison and his eight thousand attempts at perfecting the alkaline battery. Persistence demands creative thinking, and creative thinking incites initiative.

Help other people—Helping others gives you a sense of sharing, but the interaction also opens you to new ideas. When you are willing to help, you are demonstrating your capacity to listen, learn, or enlighten. Together these three qualities foster initiative.

If you want to stand out in a crowd,

you have to take a step out in front of it.

~ Unknown

Wherever you see a successful business,

someone once made a courageous decision.

~ Peter Drucker

THINK & ACT LIKE A WINNER

twelve

Guard Against
Neglect

*After a speaking engagement I once had in
Boca Raton, Florida, I was driving south
for roughly forty minutes to catch a flight
out of Miami's airport. Driving along,
I noticed a number of billboards lining the highway
I was traveling. Many caught my attention,
but one in particular stood out, and still does today.*

The ad showed an old man's picture blown up to fill the entire billboard. The wrinkled and worn face was huge, with the focus on his smile—ear to ear. The thrust of it, though, was that the man had no teeth! Big and pink were his gums, with nothing on them. The image was hilarious! The caption read, "If you neglect them long enough . . . they will eventually go away!" I laughed out loud and thought, "Well, isn't that true?!"

Mostly anything that you neglect will eventually go away. Your spouse, your job, your house, your finances, even your teeth! Everything can be gone in an instant or dwindle away over time. Is that what we want?

Some days we might wish that we didn't have to deal with certain people or problems, so we ignore them. But if we continue putting things off, how will we ever resolve them?

We need to guard against neglect in order to protect what is ours or what we are striving for.

In one of his latest articles, speaker and business philosopher Jim Rohn wrote:

People often ask me how I became successful in that six-year period of time when many of the people I knew did not. The answer is simple: The things I found to be easy to do, they found to be easy not to do. I found it easy to set the goals that could change my life. They found it easy not to. I found it easy to read the books that could affect my thinking and my ideas. They found that easy not to.

I found it easy to attend the classes and the seminars, and to get around other successful people. They said it probably really wouldn't matter. If I had to sum it up, I would say what I found to be easy to do, they found to be easy not to do. Six years later, I'm a millionaire and they are all still blaming the economy, the government, and company policies, yet they neglected to do the basic, easy things.

In fact, the primary reason most people are not doing as well as they could and should can be summed up in a single word: neglect.

It is not the lack of money—banks are full of money. It is not the lack of opportunity—America, and much of the free world, continues to offer the most unprecedented and abundant opportunities in the last six thousand years of recorded history. It is not the lack of books—libraries are full of books—and they are free! It is not the schools—the classrooms are full of good teachers. We have plenty of ministers, leaders, counselors, and advisors.

Everything we would ever need to become rich and powerful

and sophisticated is within our reach. The major reason that so few take advantage of all that we have is simply, neglect.

Neglect is like an infection. Left unchecked it will spread throughout our entire system of disciplines and eventually lead to a complete breakdown of a potentially joy-filled and prosperous human life.

Not doing the things we know we should do causes us to feel guilty and guilt leads to an erosion of self-confidence. As our self-confidence diminishes, so does the level of our activity. And as our activity diminishes, our results inevitably decline. And as our results suffer, our attitude begins to weaken. And as our attitude begins the slow shift from positive to negative, our self-confidence diminishes even more . . . and on and on it goes.

So my suggestion is that when given the choice of "easy to" and "easy not to" that you do not neglect to do the simple, basic, "easy," but potentially life-changing activities and disciplines.

When I read this, I thought, "He hit the nail right on the head!" Successful people do what others won't do. They don't neglect anything; they guard against neglect by getting things done.

How can you guard against neglect? Practice the following guidelines.

Don't put things off—Do what's hardest first. We all have certain things that we dislike but that we must do. If you make those items part of your daily routine, over time they will become just routine habits. Do them first thing in the morning to get them out of the way, and then you will be able to focus the rest of your day on the things that you like to do.

Reward yourself for getting things done—Once you complete a task that you didn't feel like doing but did anyway to guard against neglect, get up, move around, and reward yourself with a cup of coffee, a donut, or something that provides you with a small sense of merit. After all, you'll deserve it!

Don't let yourself get distracted—Get done with it instead! Create an environment that fits your work style, and you will set yourself up to avoid distractions.

Visualize—Picture what will happen if you don't do what you need to do. Perhaps you could buy a funny card that shows a toothless old man and put it on your desk to remind you of the consequences of neglect. Then imagine what will happen when you finish your dreaded task. Perhaps next to the gummy guy you can put a card showing off a white-toothed, red-lipped smile.

Remember what your ultimate goal is—Have pictures of your family, vacation, car, or hobby readily visible to remind yourself why you do what you do.

I long to accomplish a great and noble task;

but it is my chief duty and job

to accomplish humble tasks

as though they were great and noble.

The world is moved along,

not only by the mighty shoves of its heroes,

but also by the aggregate of the tiny pushes

of each honest worker.

~ Helen Keller

If I have the belief that I can do it,

I shall surely acquire the capacity to do it.

~ Mahatma Gandhi

THINK & ACT LIKE A WINNER

thirteen

Appreciation

*When you get your priorities straight,
you have nothing to worry about.*

Two years ago I was in on my way to Washington, DC. I love that city. It is full of so much history and interesting people. I can say, though, that I don't like the traffic.

I had just finished a management seminar in Baltimore and was driving down to my hotel just outside of Georgetown. There was a major accident on the freeway and traffic was at a dead stop for miles.

I had a newspaper next to me in the car so I picked it up and started reading.

The front page was covered with news about Monica Lewinsky and former President Bill Clinton. At that point, I had heard enough about the scandal and was ready for something new. I figured that if I was in Washington, DC, that they would have better news to report. It happened to be the opposite. The scandal was everywhere. I quickly put down the paper and turned on the radio. I flipped it to A.M. so that I could pick up a talk show or a ball game—something that would occupy my mind while I sat.

I tuned into a talk show that was about politics. (Can you believe that—politics in Washington?) As I listened, I became caught up in the conversation. It was the public's reaction to the scandal with the president.

The same rhetoric was going on . . . "Throw him out of office!" was one side; "It's none of our business what he does in his personal life," was the other. The discussion repeated all the old stuff I had heard for weeks—until the next caller, who really got me thinking, spoke her piece.

It was a woman. Her accent indicated that she wasn't from the United States. She quickly explained that it was extremely important that she speak. She was visiting Washington for the first time; in fact, it was the first time in her life that she had an opportunity to leave the remote village in Africa where she lived. As she began to speak, you could sense the sincerity, passion, and excitement in her voice. She told the announcer how she was in town to visit her country's embassy to lobby for aid and human rights in her country. She only had one week in the city before heading back to her village.

What caught my attention was the language she used in explaining her opinion about the situation that was making news in all the print and broadcast media. She said, "I am sickened by the United States."

"Sickened?" I thought to myself. That's a pretty descriptive word. Sickened. Why was she sickened? She could have been angry, shocked, upset, or any other word. But she used "sickened."

She said that in her country, people have to walk one mile just to get a drink of water, and when they get to the watering site, they hope that the shipment of rice has arrived so that they can feed their families. She explained that she had four children herself. Then she proclaimed that if two of them made it to adulthood, she would feel privileged.

Can you imagine losing two of your children and still feeling privileged? Not me. Yet she seemed to think that it was one of the best things that could happen to her.

What she said next really got me. "I can't believe how much of a big deal the citizens of this country are making over this situation."

Big deal? Well, yeah! The president lied under oath. He lied on television to the American public. "This is a big deal!" I thought.

Yet she was sickened by our reaction.

In her world, what was happening was so much more traumatic to any lie or scandal we could imagine. In her world, people die. People go without food. They go to bed hungry, malnourished, and disease-ridden.

She went on to say, in effect, "The reason your country is making so much of a big deal about this situation is that most Americans have nothing else to worry about! I am not saying that what your president did was right, but I am saying that I don't understand the reaction of the people who are concerned—concerned so much that they would watch TV, read papers, protest in front of buildings, and give of their time to talk to neighbors and relatives for hours about the situation. If Americans only knew that as they talked, our children are dying, going to bed hungry, and losing their parents to war and famine, then they would be sickened too! You have so much wealth and you don't even realize it!"

As I sat in my car, I became humbled immediately. I started to think of my two daughters and how much I love them. I couldn't imagine them going to bed hungry. I began to wonder if I could handle worrying about whether or not they would be strong enough to survive diseases that bombarded their tiny bodies.

I thought about the things that had recently consumed my life. When would we have enough money to move to that bigger house? I had to make sure I called ChemLawn to kill the weeds in my front yard. Did I make the right choice in staying at the Radisson in the Bahamas, or should I have chosen the Marriott? Private school for the kids is going to be over $5000 this year! Boy, do I need a new suit! I am tired of cheap suits! I must go to that expensive men's store in Georgetown when I get there. I need to trade in my two-year-old car for a new one. I wonder how my investments are doing. It'll be nice to get home and watch my new satellite TV system. Should I see a movie tonight or stay in and have room service?

Are you with me? We are so conditioned with the wealth around us that we don't even see it. We tend to focus on those things that we don't have instead of seeing the things that we do.

I pulled the world almanac out and found that the average income in the U.S. in 1998 was over $36,000, and the median average value of an American home was $129,300! What wealth we have!

If you have ever traveled to a third-world country, you know what I mean. You see dirt and congestion, poorly constructed buildings, and a lack of general resources. The technology is about ten years behind ours, and new innovation is scarce. When traveling to these kinds of places, I am amazed at how far behind they are, and I'm always glad to get back to the U.S. to see our clean streets and the majesty of our infrastructure—which almost every one of us, unfortunately, takes for granted.

Have we, the U.S., become spoiled brats? Have we forgotten how good we have it? The common saying must be true: You don't know what you have until it's gone.

When I hear employees at my seminars talk about how bad they have it, how others make more money, and why they should quit their jobs or go out on strike, I want to shake them and say, "You have nothing else to worry about!"

Following are some things you can do to remind yourself that, when you keep your priorities straight and appreciate what you have, you can make your life better.

Count your blessings—Write a list of all the things that make you happy. What advantages do you have? What are you taking for granted?

Take a drive outside of your neighborhood or regular commute—It is easy to get caught up in our own worlds. I want you to drive to a lower income side of town. Look at the houses, the yards, and the cars, if you see any. Ask yourself, "Would I want to trade?" Try to focus on what you have instead of what you don't have.

Try a different job for a day—It is easy to think that we are the only ones who must do things we don't like. Get a fresh perspective by doing, or at least imagining to do, someone else's job. You might find it humbling. For example, go to a fast-food restaurant and select a worker to observe. Watch this person and everything he or she is involved in. Do you see him pick up the ketchup-splattered tray strewn with garbage from a lazy customer, pitch the garbage in the bin, wipe down the tray, and then pick up a mop? Do you see her smile at and assist a verbally abusive customer who is complaining about too many onions and demanding a new burger after it is already half-eaten? Imagine that you are also involved in those circumstances. How do you think you would like that job?

Give! Get involved!—By searching out and observing poverty, poor conditions, and those less fortunate than you, you might end up feeling better about yourself and your personal surroundings. That's wonderful, but be careful you don't use those less fortunate as pawns in a game of self-aggrandizement. Realize how fortunate you really are and how having what you do allows you to give. You might have more leisure time than someone else—why not volunteer to teach an adult how to read? You might have more money— why not donate some to a cause you believe in?

Success

To laugh often and love much;

To win the respect of intelligent people and the

affection of children;

To earn the appreciation of honest critics

and endure the betrayal of false friends;

To appreciate beauty;

To find the best in others;

To leave the world a bit better,

Whether by a healthy child,

a garden patch, or a redeemed social condition;

To know even one life has breathed easier

because you have lived,

That is to have succeeded.

~ Ralph Waldo Emerson

THINK & ACT LIKE A WINNER

fourteen

From Whiner to Winner

Have you ever met someone who is a whiner?
You know, someone who seems to complain about
every little thing he or she can find.
Someone who might say, "I had to turn left,
and no one would let me! The traffic kept coming
and coming! Finally the light turned yellow
and one last car just HAD to speed through!
I had to wait for it, and by then, the light
had turned red! I could've been stopped for going
through a red light! I think I had the right
to smash into that car going through a yellow light
when they SAW I was trying to turn!
Some people!"

And you sit there thinking, "Well, are you a defensive driver or aren't you? If not, you better get off the road! Besides, driving is a privilege—not a right."

But before you can say a word, the person comes out with, "And you know, the coffee at the convenience store was SO stale this morning. I thought I would die!"

Has anyone really ever died from drinking stale coffee?

We have all been caught in a trap like this with someone at one time or another. What do you think a whiner like that does to your performance? It brings it down! And quickly!

As stated previously, outside elements affect our outlook. Each of us is affected by what we see, hear, and do. We have all heard this concept before, but we rarely take an honest look at the consequences of what it really means and the impact it has on our lives.

Many people associate with whiners, whether intentionally or not. By doing so, they soon find themselves being influenced by these people without even realizing it. The worst consequence of associating with whiners is that you become one too.

Truer than the saying, "Birds of a feather flock together," whether you associate yourself with positive or negative influences, you will start to develop behavior like that of the people and environment you choose to surround yourself with. It's human nature at its best.

Because of this pattern, we tend to develop certain characteristics and attitudes without even realizing it. If you try to evaluate your own behavior, you'll find that you cannot have an unbiased, objective opinion of it. Why? Because we don't see things as they are; we see things as we are. Moreover, sometimes we see things as we want to see them, not necessarily how they really are.

For example, when you hear your voice on a tape, you are usually shocked or repelled by what you hear. Many people immediately turn off the recording because they dislike the sound of their own voice. What is happening is that you are hearing your voice as others do and not as how you thought it sounded.

If we could view our actions, self-talk, and reactions to

THINK & ACT LIKE A WINNER

specific situations as we could hear an objective recording of our voice, we might be able to better understand how the pattern of picking up negative influences can slowly creep into a cycle of behavior that hurts our overall performance without our recognizing it.

Situations and events that elicit responses from us happen on a daily basis. Suppose your boss passes you over for a promotion; someone says something out of the ordinary and you don't understand why; you are cut off in traffic; you are not invited to a party; you lose a sale to your competitor; anything can happen over the course of your day. How do you respond? Most of us respond in a knee-jerk fashion, trying to control these events that occur and ending up feeling frustrated or angry.

But we need to realize that 90% of all situations cannot be controlled. The other 10% of situations we do have control over. We'd like to believe we can control 100% of everything that happens in our lives, but in reality, we can't. Ultimately, we can only respond to, not control, 90% of the situations we find ourselves in.

Therefore, since the majority of the events that occur are outside of our control, we don't want to focus on how we can gain control of them. Instead, we want to focus on what we can control—our response to these situations. We can control how we view and handle the situations in our lives.

It's like the saying, "When life hands you lemons, make lemonade." What you do in response to a negative situation is what determines how far you'll go in life.

For example, if you are passed over for a promotion at work, regardless of why or how, know that the deed is done and it's up to you to decide how to respond to, not control, the situation. Will you speak to your boss about what you can do in the future to improve your chances for advancement? Or will you go to your boss demanding that he or she look at all you've already done, which you think proves you should have received the promotion? Which response would actually improve your chances of getting a better position when one becomes available?

The clearest way to break a behavioral pattern is to understand the following five-stage sequence representing the logic and reasoning behind how we perform.

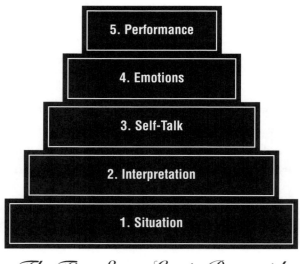

The Five-Stage Logic Pyramid

THINK & ACT LIKE A WINNER

Let's take a hypothetical situation and run it through the above program of behavior. Each stage is based upon the previous behavior building up to the performance peak.

1. **Situation**—Suppose you lose a sale to a competitor, not as a result of something you did or failed to do, but simply because the customer chose to go with another vendor. The loss is something that you could not have controlled. After you receive the news, you immediately begin to interpret the situation.

2. **Interpretation**—Is your interpretation positive or negative? If it's positive, you might see the situation as an opportunity to learn more about the competition. If it's negative, you might see the situation as unfair.

3. **Self-Talk**—The slant of your interpretation determines the slant of your self-talk, or how you will go over the situation in your head. If you are like the average person, you would probably interpret the given situation negatively, which would lead to negative self-talk. Instead of thinking, "Hey, that's OK. There are plenty of other customers to whom I can sell," you might start to doubt your sales ability, question whether or not your product is good, or wonder if your product is overpriced. We will take a closer look at the effects of self-talk momentarily, but know that your self-talk, positive or negative, infiltrates your feelings and determines how you feel.

4. **Emotions**—Your emotions are fragile, uncontrollable, and influenced by the thoughts running through your mind. If you interpret this situation positively and your self-talk involves thinking of the next opportunity, you will probably feel content or pleased to know that you didn't do anything wrong or neglect to do something right in this situation.

You'll tend to be upbeat calling on your next potential customer. But if your self-talk involved rationalizing why you failed or doubts about your ability or product, then you will probably feel depressed, defeated, or angry. If you don't retreat into paperwork, you'll be more inclined to face your next potential customer feeling uncertain instead of confident.

5. **Performance**—Whether you're feeling self-assured or inadequate, your emotions affect your performance. If you feel the former, you'll forge ahead with your next sales call. If the latter, you might retreat into paperwork. These sample behaviors are direct results of the chain of events we have examined. Since we already stated that the average person would interpret the above situation negatively and run negative self-talk through his or her mind, we also know that this average person will be feeling negatively and therefore will act negatively. Why? As children, we learn very quickly to avoid anything that feels uncomfortable. If you touch a hot stove and it burns you, you learn not to do it again. Likewise, if you lose a sale and you experience a negative feeling, you are more likely to avoid that rejection again.

If the same or a similar situation were to occur again, you would tend to draw on your experience of what has happened before. If you previously responded positively, you will tend to respond well again. If you previously responded negatively, you will tend to fear the new situation, most likely without any reason except your own feelings of fear. Either way, the cycle continues with each similar situation that may occur in your life. Knowing this, do you want to begin interpreting situations positively so that all subsequent stages lead to high performance? Do you want to go from being a whiner to a winner?

THINK & ACT LIKE A WINNER

I want to examine the notion of self-talk in more detail because its effects can be so dramatic on our emotional and physical well being.

To illustrate my point, picture yourself standing alone at the base of a newly constructed skyscraper. You are about to take a tour of the structure's penthouse suite. After waiting a few minutes, a man in a doorman's uniform appears from the building and escorts you directly to the lobby elevator. He presses button number 70, the top floor.

Once the elevator reaches its stop, the door opens and you see directly into the master office suite. It is exquisite! Your guide motions you into the suite. Every detail seems to be in place . . . the lush carpet beneath your shoes, the contemporary-style desk, the minimalist décor, and especially the glass walls that expose the beautiful skyline of the city and the horizon that stretches for miles. As you are looking out, you suddenly notice to the far right a group of workers outside on the balcony. They are constructing the railing.

You look around for the doorman, but he has gone. So you walk toward the balcony and slide open the door. Immediately a rush of air whooshes into your face. One of the workers looks up at you, but turns back to her work. You step out onto the concrete and close the door behind you. A cold and blustery wind turns the lower half of your overcoat into a flap-machine, which you hold down with your hands in your pockets. Balancing carefully, you decide to take off your socks and shoes, throw them near the door, and feel the icy cold concrete under your feet. Hands back in pockets, you walk toward the edge of the balcony. You hold your head high, breathe in deeply, admire the view in front of you, and instinctively curl your toes over the edge of the balcony. Then your eyes move downward. You quickly bow your head down and see nothing but cold air between you and the city below.

All right, how do you feel? Nervous? Are your hands sweaty? Did you grimace? Feel a chill? Has your heart sunk to your stomach? Did you at least move around in your seat?

The reason for this experiment is to illustrate the power of self-talk and how your mind affects the way you feel while it takes in information. The amazing part is that you don't even have to experience the act—you just have to think about it—and your mind creates feelings that make your emotions and body respond instinctively.

If you experienced any of the effects described above, what do you think are the emotional and physical effects of negative self-talk? How do you think it affects performance?

Your emotions and your body respond to stimuli that you have entertained in your brain. Negative self-talk usually brings anti-productive results; it summons negative feelings that block out happiness, excitement, or concentration. Your body then reacts to those emotions in various ways, such as sweaty palms, sick stomach, or nervous ticks like shaking your leg. When you are not feeling well emotionally or physically, how well do you think your performance will be?

The only way to control these effects is to stop the negative information that is causing them! You might not be able to control a feeling of terror or a bodily twitch, but you can control the self-talk that produces them. Positive self-talk is a mental process that you can use to promote positive emotions and physical reactions, and thereby promote peak performance.

It is important to understand the true effect of negative

THINK & ACT LIKE A WINNER

stimuli on performance. We often tend to be our own worst enemy, sending negative thoughts and emotions into our system which, in turn, foster poor performance. Isn't that the opposite of what you want? The key is to have a positive interpretation of uncontrollable situations from the beginning, to believe that people are inherently good no matter what the situation is.

If you want to win, it is important to understand that whiners and their negativity will adversely affect your performance, and ultimately, your life. Wellness begets wellness. Positivity breeds positivity. It's a simple enough formula: Surround yourself with the best, and that's exactly what you'll get and what you'll exude.

We cannot tell what may happen to us

in the strange medley of life.

But we can decide what happens in us,

how we take it,

what we do with it—

and that is what really counts in the end.

~ Joseph Fort Newton

THINK & ACT LIKE A WINNER

Character cannot be developed in ease and quiet.

Only through experience of trial and suffering

can the soul be strengthened,

vision cleared,

ambition inspired,

and success achieved.

~ Helen Keller

THINK & ACT LIKE A WINNER

fifteen

Search for
Greatness

*In a conversation I had the other day with a
Japanese mother-to-be, as we talked
about life and the ever-changing world,
I asked her an important question
that took her by surprise. I asked her what word
she would pick for her child if she had only one word
to choose: a word that would stick with the child
for life; a word that would define what the child's
life would be; a word that would define the child's
activities, talents, and accomplishments.
What word would she choose?*

She paused for a second and said, "Success. I want my child to be successful."

As I made reference to earlier in this book, "we only know what we know," and from what I know of the Japanese culture, they are driven culturally to succeed. Think of the products you buy from Japan. Are they of the best quality, or do you find yourself returning their products regularly? Are you like me, willing to pay more for their products because you know from experience the quality that you can expect?

The Japanese tend to sacrifice their personal happiness to create a successful society. I am generalizing, of course, but think about it: don't many of them live in closed, cramped quarters? Ride buses and trams to work? Send their kids to school year round? Go to school 10 hours a day, six days a week? Work 60-hour work weeks rather than our 40?

Why do they do these things? Is it because they wish to be more successful?

If you were to ask a mother-to-be from the U.S., what life-word do you think she would choose for her child? From what I know of American culture, she most likely would choose the word, "happiness." She would want her child to be happy. Why? As a culture (again, in general), we do everything with one thing in mind: to be as happy as possible. We even teach it in our schools, as our Declaration of Independence promotes each citizen's unalienable right to "the pursuit of Happiness."

What are the things that do or would make you happy? Rolling over and going back to sleep in the morning? Not having to follow rules or the direction of others? Having all of your time to yourself? Not having to commit to anyone or anything? Not having to pay bills, have a job, or listen to anyone criticize you?

Is it possible that our lust for happiness keeps us from achieving our goals? I think so, because to be successful, one has to sacrifice, focus, and follow rules. These things might not bring us happiness, but they are ingredients in a recipe for success.

I don't know about you, but if my wife were about to deliver a child into this world, I don't think "success" or "happiness" would be the life-word that I would choose for

THINK & ACT LIKE A WINNER

our child. I am not saying that I wouldn't want the child to be successful, and I am certainly not saying that I wouldn't want him or her to be happy. I would choose the word, "great," because if the child is GREAT, both success and happiness will come to him or her.

I think there is more to life than sacrificing everything for success or chasing happiness. I want my kids to be great parents, great co-workers, great musicians, great community leaders, great teachers, and great citizens, regardless how successful or happy society thinks they need to be.

I have met many successful individuals in my time, and I have also seen the results of those people who live just to be happy. In both cases, I have seen downfalls in their lives, but I have also met some great individuals . . . great teachers, great athletes, great givers . . . and those are the people I treasure the most.

Let me share with you a story. It might sound simple, but its meaning illustrates my point.

My kids love Walt Disney films, and because they are young, they seem to like to watch the same film over and over. I, on the other hand, have very few movies that I like to watch more than once. One evening, my girls got their way and we watched the movie Hercules for the ninetieth time. Finally, the story seemed to speak to me about the struggles of life.

The story begins with Hercules (the newborn child of the god Zeus) being stolen from his parents and transported to Earth, where he was to be made mortal so he could be killed. Hercules did not fully ingest the potion that was needed to accomplish this, so he retained powers that normal humans would never experience.

A couple found Hercules on the side of a road and raised him as their child. All throughout his childhood, Hercules knew he was different. He didn't fit in with other children; he was always stumbling or banging into and destroying something. But inside he felt he was destined for something great—he just didn't know what.

One day his adoptive father explained to Hercules how he had been found and that he was from some place else. It explained why he didn't seem to fit in.

Hercules decided to find out where and what he was supposed to be. He sought out a statue of his true father and asked it what he was to do. The statue came to life and told Hercules that he was to become a hero. Once he achieved that, he would be turned into a god and could return to his family in the heavens. Hercules set out to be a hero with much enthusiasm and desire.

His enthusiasm is much like that of a new employee on the job . . . anxious, willing to learn, and excited about the journey ahead.

Hercules believed that if he became the most successful gladiator, then he would become a hero and god. So he hired a coach and trained as hard as he could. He was willing to do whatever it took to be a hero, driven by the idea of success as a gladiator.

Isn't this true with many of us? We are driven to be successful. In our jobs, in our neighborhoods, and in our families, we search out the praises of success. We long to hear words like, "Oh John, he is so successful," or, "Wow, Mary and Joe sure have a successful marriage, don't they?"

But what about greatness?

Hercules sought out success, and he was successful. He became the most successful gladiator in the world, but he didn't become a god. All the success in the world did not get him where he wanted to be.

Discouraged, tired, and exasperated, Hercules was ready to give up. He had done everything that he was told. He had traveled from town to town, conquering monster after monster. He was successful, no doubt about it—no one could beat him. But he felt empty inside. He thought success would be different, greater, grander, more fulfilling. But now he felt unsure. He knew that he was the most successful of any gladiator, yet he still wasn't a god.

He decided that being a successful gladiator was not as important as achieving happiness, and he became obsessed with the idea. He wanted to have fun. He thought being the most popular person in all the land would give him the respect of his peers and turn him into a hero among men. He began buying castles and throwing fancy parties. He had statues built in his honor. He developed a full clothing line bearing his name, including shoes and hats. Everywhere he went, people admired him. They wanted his autograph. He was feeling happy, yet, it wasn't good enough to satisfy his destiny.

Hercules was a searcher. He was searching for something better, bigger. More than success or happiness, he wanted to be a god! That was his destiny.

Meg was happy and successful until it came time for her to pay her debt. Hercules was angry that Meg had to give her soul to Hades, yet it was out of his hands. As Hercules said goodbye to Meg, he realized that nothing else mattered to him but her. He shouted to Hades, "Take my life for hers. Without Meg, my life means nothing!" And so Hades obliged and released Meg. At that moment, when Hercules grabbed Meg's hand to pull her from the pit, he became a true hero, whose greatness came through in an act of love. Thus, he was turned into a god.

The story of Hercules reminds me of other searchers in life. These people are willing take to risks to find their path and search for something greater. They are never satisfied with being who they are or what they do because they believe in ongoing improvement.

Searchers also have an inner burning—the type that keeps them up through the night figuring out with excitement and joy how to get and keep the fire going. They know they are here for something more than what they have or what they are doing. They always search for more out of life.

Searchers use the characteristics in this book to practice lives of searching. They apply creativity, demonstrate charisma, and more to lead themselves down the path to something better, down the path to greatness.

Are you a searcher? Do you search out greatness? Have you ever told yourself that you are destined to be great? Most of us have not. We don't want the criticism or work associated with this task. We usually take the comfortable road.

But it's not too late to take the off ramp and travel another route. If you know deep inside that you are destined for something great, even if you don't know what it is, start your search today.

THINK & ACT LIKE A WINNER

ABCs of Success

A   Apply yourself wholeheartedly—every moment

B   Become your dream

C   Choose greatness—which is beyond happiness

D   Dare to be all that you desire

E   Evaluate your success daily

F   Fill your mind, office, and home with inspiration

G   Grow through your mistakes

H   Honor that you have choices

I   Initiate contact—smile

J   Jump through hoops

K   Keep learning—every person is a teacher

L   Love your work

M   Move toward total health

N   Negotiate wisely

O   Open your mind to all possibilities

P   Practice patience

Q	Quiet your mind
R	Reprogram your negatives into positives
S	Set goals daily
T	Tip poor customer service—through speaking up!
U	Under every rock lies a foundation
V	Validate your fears—then conquer them!
W	Whisper loving thoughts to your partner
X	X-plain your ideas—out loud!
Y	Yield to others' thoughts before you make recommendations
Z	Zero in on excellence

~ Heather Swanson

THINK & ACT LIKE A WINNER

I am not the smartest or most talented person

in the world, but I succeeded

because I keep going, and going, and going.

~ Sylvester Stallone

THINK & ACT LIKE A WINNER

s i x t e e n

Tell the
Truth

Truth: 1. *a statement proven to be or accepted as true*
2. *sincerity, integrity, or reality*

Why have I included a chapter on truth? How much impact does telling the truth really have on our lives?

I believe that by learning to be honest and forthright with ourselves and others, we can change our lives!

Being honest is critical to business success in many ways. When you are honest about both the good things and the bad things, you build trust and confidence in your business relationships.

Have you ever stretched the truth or withheld information from others? How did it make you feel? What type of emotional stress did it cause you? I hope you are not still doing it. When people practice dishonesty for a long time, their lies seem to become the truth to them. When that happens, they tend to become less emotionally sensitive, and soon only the big lies make them feel nervous or uncomfortable. A liar's ability to empathize with the person to whom he or she has lied diminishes to the point where the relationship must necessarily suffer. In other words, the more one lies to other people, the less one is able to relate to them.

Why do we lie in the first place? Could it be that we are not satisfied with our current reality? Do we like to create another image of ourselves? Are we creating an illusory life that seems better if only in our minds?

The problem with creating a false image is that it is a manifestation of a negative belief about ourselves—we pretend we are better than we believe ourselves to be. Telling an untruth further convinces us that we are not good enough, which leads to low self-esteem and ultimately low performance. Is this what we want?

A recent USA Today poll found that only 56% of Americans teach honesty to their children. A Louis Harris poll states that 65% of high-school students would cheat on an important exam. In the 1997 nationwide survey, "The Day America Told the Truth," 93% of Americans admitted that they lie "regularly and habitually" at work. Are we becoming a nation that is slipping deeper into a cycle of lies? Are lies becoming an acceptable form of reality? I hope not!

I wouldn't be considered a good father if I failed to tell my daughter the consequences of her lying. Suppose she told me that she did not take the last few cookies in the cookie jar when I could see the crumbs around her mouth and in the empty jar. I would need to scold her and teach her the value of being honest. I would also encourage her to look at what she could do differently the next time she wants a cookie instead of focusing on her negative behaviors of stealing and lying.

I also wouldn't be considered a good manager if I didn't communicate honestly with my employees and expect the same from them. The truth eventually appears, and any previously told lies or concealment of information would ultimately backfire, causing damage to the company's success. Likewise, instead of pretending or "fudging" our way through a difficult situation at work, we must learn to ask for help. By doing so, we build and grow our relationships.

In 1982, The Forum Corporation of Boston, Massachusetts, studied 341 salespeople from eleven different companies in five different industries. Their goal was to determine what accounted for the difference between top producers and below-average producers. The results were predictable. Skills, knowledge, and charisma were the standout characteristics of the top performers. But most importantly, all of the top performers said that they believe honesty was the leading characteristic that led to their successes.

When customers trust their salesperson, they are more likely to buy from him or her again and again—even when the prices are higher. They'd much rather hear a salesperson admit to and resolve a problem than hear the salesperson make excuses or shift the blame to someone else.

Have you heard the saying, "What comes around goes around?" I believe that what we give out comes back to us two-fold. If you find your business isn't where you want or expect it to be, your salary isn't as high as you'd like, or your relationship with your partner or children isn't how you'd like it to be, then consider your behaviors. Are you taking ownership of your action or inaction? When you do, you can begin to speak your truths with passion and confidence. When you speak your truth, you honor yourself. By honoring yourself, you honor others in the process.

Honesty does pay off in your favor, which is why it's vitally important to establish a pattern of honesty in your life. Lying only hurts your chances of success in every relationship, whether it's with customers, co-workers, family members, or friends. Even if you think that telling a lie doesn't bother you, your subconscious mind knows it does and places the guilt and shame in other areas of your life. At some level, you always know when you are deceiving yourself or others. Feelings of guilt or shame arise, and your conscience steps in to guide you in the right direction, the honest direction.

If these feelings don't arise, don't be fooled into thinking you're a capable liar who can get away with it! Your brain knows the truth! It will express those feelings somehow, perhaps subconsciously, such as through a part of your body. For example, you might experience a headache or a pain in your shoulder or back for no apparent reason. But these aches and pains could very well be your mind telling you to take a closer look at your intentions and actions.

You might not be telling an outright lie, but perhaps you are making excuses instead of digging deeper for the true meaning or reality of a situation. I know how easy it can be to fall into such a trap of dishonesty. For a short time during the growth of my seminar business, there was a lull in activity. Many people at work and at home wondered if the business would even survive. I gave many excuses as to why business was slow, using the same rationales that most unsuccessful salespeople do. These included, "The economy is down," and, "It's summertime and budgets are tight until the end of the year." Perhaps an excuse even happened to be true—I mean, it was summer.

But I wasn't being honest with myself, or with those who were concerned. When I finally looked deeper, I saw the

THINK & ACT LIKE A WINNER

reality of the situation: the business was doing poorly because I wasn't making the calls that I needed to be making. I was working long hours, caught up in the administrative side of the business, but I was not putting enough time and effort into the marketing side.

I decided it was time to break the cycle I was in, take ownership of my action and inaction, and take responsibility for my success and my failure.

I got creative! I typed up a sign and hung it next to my telephone. It read, "Your business is slow because you're not doing what's needed. Make the calls!" I couldn't help but look at it every day. Since it was right by my phone, it was clearly visible for a good 90% of the day. It's a simple strategy that worked for me then and continues to work for me today.

It now seems as though I have signs everywhere! Next to my alarm clock is a sign that sports the phrase, "Interested or committed?" When I see that sign, I ask myself if I am interested in growing my business or if I am committed to growing my business. If I were just interested, I would sit and ponder possibilities, but when I am committed, I get up and get going. It's as simple as that.

This process has helped to keep me on task as well as to keep me forthright in my business endeavors. Such a reality check drives my motivation to succeed. In fact, being honest about the reality of a situation is the best dose of motivation I can give myself.

How many of us ignore the truth or reality of a situation? Instead of being honest with ourselves, we often tend to rationalize why things are the way they are—because it seems our self-esteem can't take the truth. Perhaps that's why the phrase, "We don't see things the way they are; we see things as we are," rings so true.

Research shows that, in general, people want to believe what they are told, even if it's an outlandish lie. Why? Perhaps because of a basic need to trust or believe in the honesty of others. Unfortunately, many people tell others what they want to hear rather than speaking the truth, which is what they need to hear.

What does it take for you to be honest with yourself and with others? The first step is recognizing when you're not being honest with yourself. Then be willing to look beyond excuses for real reasons. Listen to your instincts and intuition, as we've discussed in a previous chapter. Pay attention to what your mind and body try to tell you. These powerful tools will help you learn to adjust your behavior so that you think and act like a winner. When you learn to be honest with yourself, you build confidence, and with confidence, you won't find it necessary to be dishonest with other people in your life.

When you break yourself of the habit of being dishonest to yourself and others, you find that you are more emotionally free, even though the pain of the truth may hurt. Be kind to yourself in the process. Too much effort can sometimes cause such resistance that your attempts at improving may be short lived. Honor your shortcomings and focus on changing the experience in the future. Let the past go and move forward in the here and now.

If things feel like they're getting out of control, I invite you to read the following poem, which I found on the Internet (unfortunately, the author is unknown).

THINK & ACT LIKE A WINNER

You Can Never Hide From Yourself

I have to live with myself, and so,
I want to be fit for myself to know.
I want to be able, as days go by,
Always to look myself straight in the eye.
I don't want to stand, with the setting sun,
And hate myself for the things I have done.
I want to go out with my head erect,
I want to deserve all men's respect.
For here in the struggle for fame and self
I want to be able to like myself.
I don't want to look at myself and know
I'm bluster, a bluff, and an empty show.
I never can hide myself from ME.
I see what others may never see.
I know what others may never know;
I never can fool myself, and so,
Whatever happens, I want to be
Self respecting and conscience free
When you rationalize,
you do just that.
You make rational lies.

~ Author Unknown

*Those who exaggerate in their statements
belittle themselves.*

~ C. Simmons

To be persuasive, we must be believable.

To be believable, we must be credible.

To be credible, we must be truthful.

~ Edward R. Murrow

THINK & ACT LIKE A WINNER

seventeen

If it's Meant to Be, then it's Up to Me

*Coming from a sales background,
I am very familiar with the phrase, "If it's meant
to be, then it's up to me!" Sales managers all over the
country utter these words on a daily basis.*

E ven though my first boss practiced the "repetition in learning" method with me, repeating the phrase over and over again, I didn't understand the gravity of it until I started my own business. Now I have a true appreciation for the concept that the phrase explains. Unfortunately, too many of us have yet to learn what it really means.

My first taste of this understanding came at the first motivational seminar I ever attended. A series of top speakers from around the country congregated to produce a success seminar. My boss at the time thought it was a wise investment to send his staff to this all-day event. I remember thinking to myself, "I can make more money for the company if I didn't have to attend this silly meeting. I'm making the boss good money—what do I need with a seminar on success? I'm already on top!" But of course, I had to go as part of my job.

One of the first speakers was a man named Brian Tracy. Even though I didn't find his presentation very interesting, I was captured by one of his points. He said that we are all ultimately self-employed. At first, this idea didn't make much sense to me, because I worked for a company that told me what to do. I reasoned that since I followed the guidance and direction of the company, and I got paid by the company to do so, that I wasn't self-employed. Mr. Tracy said that each of us is in control of what we do, and he added that we should go home and imagine an "Inc." after our name in our checkbook. This act would, in turn, make us think like an entrepreneur.

The philosophy was to illustrate that we all make choices. We decide for whom we work, where to live, and what career path to take. No one has control over our destiny but us.

I then realized that this way of thinking fell in line with the phrase, "If it's meant to be, then it's up to me."

One of the biggest mistakes that you can make is to believe that you work for someone else. You own and operate a business called Labor. You choose your business's area of expertise. Will it be accounting, medicine, or insurance? How about a form of engineering? Or perhaps fine or performing arts? You can change your expertise at any time because you have the freedom to choose what you do for a living.

Once you choose your area of expertise and gain the required set of skills to practice it, you then put together a resume, introduce your business to the work world, and market it to institutions.

After an employer has decided to purchase your labor (or has decided that his or her company wants to hire you for your expertise), you move on to the negotiation stage. When you negotiate your salary, you are determining what you are going to charge for your expertise. Consultants regularly

THINK & ACT LIKE A WINNER

must negotiate fees, but employees also need to keep their negotiating skills sharp. Benefits and perks may or may not be negotiable, but if you want something that a potential employer does not offer, you have the freedom to seek out other companies who do offer what you want.

An employer who hires you owes you nothing beyond what you have negotiated. Your employer is simply a customer that is paying for a product (your expertise) via your weekly paycheck. Companies work hard to retain and impress customers. Are you doing that with your employer or boss? Do you see how, "If it's meant to be, it's up to me," is true?

I have met many people who desire success at work. They want to be known as the best at what they do. But when they fall short of their expectations, they resort to "the blame game." Instead of taking responsibility for their actions, they choose to focus on what others have done to make their business—Labor—fail. They blame customers, the economy, the boss, or the employing company's policies and procedures. Slowly they sink into a rut of negativity and excuses.

But those who develop the mindset of the self-employed experience a freedom and success that others can only dream of. Why? Because they make themselves responsible for every activity that happens. That doesn't mean taking control of situations; it means responding to them. These people know that they are in charge of their own lives and are ultimately responsible for any further development. Individuals like this are successful because they take aggressive action in directing their future. They understand the rules and they play by them well and honestly.Following are some suggestions to assist you in developing a self-employed mentality.

If you don't like your job, remind yourself daily that you don't have to be there—You choose where you sell your expertise. If you are more concerned about paying bills than about looking for a different employer, then you are basically telling yourself that you think your salary is a fair representation of what your expertise is worth. That's fine, but remember that what you negotiate is what you get—your employer owes you nothing extra. If you really don't think you are getting a fair price for your expertise, look for another buyer.

What others think is not as important as what you think—Formulate your own thoughts. Don't let adversity or negative peer groups run you or your life. You will never advance or be treated as a vital connection if you blend in with the masses. Let your own thoughts guide your own actions.

Understand and believe that whatever you want, you can get—This is not just "wishful thinking." Wishes don't come true if all you do is think about them. You need to take action, too. In many cases, you simply have to ask for what you want. Other wishes take more effort. But don't allow yourself to think that only others can have success. You can too—make your own success!

Write a life plan—Average people spend more time planning their vacations and their weekends than they do their future. But think of this: people depend on you and you have liabilities. How can you meet these obligations without a plan? Write down your plan, and don't wait! Record your strengths and weaknesses. Record what you are doing now to make yourself happy. Record what you could be doing to improve your life. Then do it! If you can map out a plan for your vacation or weekend, you can do it for your life.

THINK & ACT LIKE A WINNER

Create meaningful work—Know why you are doing what you're doing. If it is for money only, you will ultimately be left feeling common and empty. But you are unique, and what you choose to do must be important to you! Take ownership of your actions. Make sure you are making the right choices for the right reasons. And most importantly, if you are not having fun or finding meaning in the effort you put forth, stop the direction you're going in and re-chart your course. Life is too short to spend it doing something that is meaningless to you. Make whatever work you do meaningful to you, and you will know the joy of working for yourself.

Yes I Can!

If you think you are beaten, you are,

If you think you dare not, you don't.

If you'd like to win, but think you can't,

It's almost certain you won't.

If you think you'll lose, you're lost,

For out in the world we find,

Success begins with a fellow's will,

It's all in the state of mind.

If you think you are outclassed, you are,

You've got to think high to rise.

You've got to be sure of yourself before

You can ever win a prize.

Life's battles don't always go

To the stronger or faster man,

But sooner or later, the person who wins,

Is the person who thinks he can!-

~ Anonymous

THINK & ACT LIKE A WINNER

Dream no small dreams

for they have no power to move men.

~ Johann Wolfgang von Goethe

Give your positive emotions a job.

~ Ralph M. Ford

Mrs. Fields Recipe for Success

Love what you're doing.

Believe in your product.

Select good people.

~ Debbi Fields

THINK & ACT LIKE A WINNER

eighteen

Vocabulary

Have you ever worried about how you look in the morning before going to work, school, or play? The worry comes from the desire to make a good impression. When you care about how you look and take the time to present yourself in a manner that makes you feel good, that good feeling radiates to others. The impression they get corresponds with how you feel. If you dress for success and feel confident, others will perceive you as successful and confident. One key ingredient in how you present yourself is easily overlooked, and that is your vocabulary.

Spend some time thinking about the vocabulary you use when you communicate with other people. Whether you are speaking or writing, the words you choose directly reflect who and what you are. Vocabulary is like clothes for your mind. I ask you now, are you truly dressing for success?

It may be unfortunate, but we are judged by how we speak. For example, if you use the vocabulary of a student, others might judge you as being young and inexperienced. If you use the vocabulary of a "slick willy," you might be judged as cunning and untrustworthy. If you use the vocabulary of a tired, jaded old-timer, you could be judged as a has-been. If you use the vocabulary of a blue-collar worker, you may be judged as unsuitable for the executive suite.

If you want to impress somebody, do it with more than just your appearance. Your speech, pronunciation, enunciation, the words you choose, and how you articulate yourself are all important factors in making a powerful first impression.

Believe it or not, successful people have their own vocabulary. The vocabulary of success mimics the qualities found in the thought processes of successful people.

If your ambition is to be a professional success, you not only have to dress the part, but your vocabulary has to be "dressed" for the part as well. The wonderful thing about vocabulary is that you can always improve it, and quite easily at that! It does not matter if you weren't blessed with the verbiage of a fast-track professional. It doesn't matter what your family, academic, social, or professional background is. What matters is that if you desire to enhance your vocabulary, you can.

When I was eighteen years old, I went through what my parents called a "figuring-out-what-I-am-going-to-do-with-my-life" stage. Hoping to break me out of it, my father gave me an Earl Nightingale audio-cassette program. I listened to it half-heartedly, because I didn't think at the time that "educational stuff" was important. Consequently, I didn't pay much attention to what I was hearing. Why? Because I already knew everything; after all, I was eighteen!

But I do recall one thing from that program (Can you imagine—five hours of taped messages and all I remember is one thing?!). The tape was discussing the top characteristics of CEOs to determine the leading factors for success. Ideas

THINK & ACT LIKE A WINNER

of what the most important characteristic could be ran through my mind: a Harvard education, a rich family, being highly motivated, or even just the good luck of being in the right place at the right time.

Although a lot of those were indeed characteristics that lent themselves to success, I had never even considered what turned out to be the most universal characteristic: vocabulary! I was amazed to think that, of all the characteristics highly successful people possess, a good vocabulary was number one. Why?

You need to have the ability to communicate your message effectively and succinctly. If you have an important message but are unable to communicate it, then you are just as hindered as someone who has no message at all.

Have you ever met someone who had a powerful vocabulary? Were they smart, or did you just think they were? You really can't tell, can you? I'm not saying that those who have a high vocabulary aren't smart or are only pretending to be. I'm saying that their vocabulary shows they're competent enough to express their views in an intelligent manner.

Here's another way to look at it. When I talk to a financial planner or broker for the first time, the person must prove his or her competence to me. I might already know the planner's credentials or accept the recommendation from the broker's brother-in-law, but when I meet the person myself, I want to know if she really knows her stuff or if he's in the wrong business. One way for me to ascertain the person's competence is to observe his or her language and ability to communicate effectively. Does he sound like he knows what he's talking about? Or is she just throwing buzzwords at me to make it look like she knows?

To illustrate my point further, let me give you an example. A recent TV commercial for an online trading company shows a band rehearsing. As the band develops a new song, one member asks, "What is a word that rhymes with 'elation?'" A few of the other members chime in with words like "temptation" and "jubilation," until drummer Ringo Starr ends the search by spouting off words like, "dividend participation," "asset allocation," and "market globalization." Everyone in the room stops what they're doing and stares at him—they are astounded at his intelligence! The narrator then states that this online trading company has created a new kind of investor: a smart investor. The impression the commercial makes is that if you invest with this company, you will be transformed into someone who is smart about his or her investments.

This commercial demonstrates that those around you, whether you know them or not, routinely judge you by the vocabulary that you use. Sometimes just knowing buzzwords is enough, but you can't fake your way through life (see the chapter on truth). You actually need to know and understand the terminology associated with what it is you are speaking about.

Where are you with your vocabulary? How do you sound? How is your enunciation, pronunciation, and grammar? I am always taken aback when I hear someone use a word improperly, but I'm even more so when I see an impeccably dressed professional talking like a stereotypical construction worker. What kind of first impression does that person make?

Furthermore, first impressions don't get do-overs. You will never get another opportunity to replace the first time you interact with a customer or potential employer.

THINK & ACT LIKE A WINNER

Do you remember the movie Educating Rita? A great deal of time and energy was spent making sure Rita was well-educated and mannerly, but also well-spoken. There's a lesson there for all of us.

When lecturing, I often direct a series of questions to my audience. The first is, "How many of you want to be more successful?" The second is, "How many of you want to make more money?" The third is, "How many of you want to be better today than you were yesterday?" The overwhelming response on all three questions is an outstanding 100%. While everyone desires all three, it is important to develop a plan to achieve these goals, to develop a blueprint to success. Desire is only half the battle. As the saying goes, "Success is 10% inspiration and 90% perspiration." Working on your vocabulary needs to be an important part of your blueprint for success.

If you are truly committed to improving your vocabulary, following are some ideas that may help.

Go to your local bookstore and buy a vocabulary tape set—That's a simple enough chore, and there are many programs from which to choose. Make sure your tape is easy on your ears and that it groups words into categories so that you will retain the information more easily. Listen to your tapes over and over, and do it regularly. Too many people listen to one tape and then move on to the next. Don't make that mistake. Master one tape before moving on to the next. Remember, anything that is repeated over and over aids in your retention.

Buy a "word" calendar—Some calendars introduce a new word and its definition for each day; some provide a new word and its definition for each week. Whichever type you buy, try using the new word throughout the day or once a day for an entire week. Yes, use the words you learn!

Subscribe to a new-word-a-day or new-word-a-week email service— Search at a search engine for keywords such as "word-a-day newsletter" or "build vocabulary via email." Again, use the words that the service introduces to you.

Read—The more you read, the better you will comprehend and understand new words, because often you can pick up the meaning of an unfamiliar term by the context in which it is used. However, keep a dictionary on hand when you read to look up those words that don't make sense.

Do it!—Make vocabulary-building a priority in your day-to-day schedule. Yes, daily! Turn off the music on your commute and listen to your tapes. Take a minute to look up a word. Read that email instead of deleting it. Remember, successful people do what others won't do.

THINK & ACT LIKE A WINNER

There are no shortcuts to any place worth going.

~ Beverly Sills

Nurture your mind with great thoughts,

for you will never go any higher than you think.

~ Benjamin Disraeli

THINK & ACT LIKE A WINNER

n i n e t e e n

Do Over

When I was a child I loved to play outdoors. Most afternoons, my buddies and I would gather in my backyard to play kickball. For anyone who might not be familiar with the game, or for those who might not remember, kickball is identical to baseball with a couple of exceptions: you use a large rubber ball instead of a baseball, you kick the ball with your foot rather than hit it with a bat, and you throw the ball at and hit a person who is off base instead of just tagging the person or base.

As I remember back to my days as a kid playing kickball in the backyard, everything seemed to be so good. My friends and I always had fun. Even if we had minor problems and difficulties, we never let them bother us too much.

One day on the field, I kicked a long fly ball to centerfield. Jim, who was not known to be the best of outfielders, missed the catch. He was, however, good at accurately throwing the ball. Jim threw the ball in my direction in an attempt to hit me before I got to the base. Well, my team thought I made it to the base safely. Jim's team didn't agree.

An argument broke out. My team was yelling, "He's safe!

He's safe!" while the other team was yelling, "He's out! He's out!" The yelling grew louder as everyone gathered at the pitcher's mound.

Then, without even a slight hint of direction, the players started singing in unison, "Do over . . . Do over . . . Do over . . . ."

It was so simple. When we couldn't resolve a conflict, we simply called for a do-over. What's that? It's the name for the process of doing something over, of course!

How many of us get so wrapped up in our failures that we can't see a single thing that will help? Sometimes, all we need is a do-over. Just forget about what's over and done with, and start afresh.

Your past is history, the future a mystery, and today a gift—that's why we call it the present. When you do something and the result is not what you want, call for a do-over.

THINK & ACT LIKE A WINNER

There are no secrets to success.

It is the result of preparation, hard work, learning

from failure.

~ General Colin L. Powell

He who is afraid of doing too much,

Always does too little.

~ German Proverb

THINK & ACT LIKE A WINNER

t w e n t y

Beware of the Golden Handcuffs

How many times have you found yourself sitting with friends or family and the topic of the ultimate dream job comes up? Your conversation goes into great detail and planning about how you would enter into this exciting career. For some, it involves moving to a sunny location. For others, it is starting their own business. For many, it involves the hobby they love the most.

But dream jobs most often stay in dreams. Why is it that we torture ourselves every day doing things that we hate to do? When I ask this question the response is usually, "Well, I don't hate my job. I just wish I was doing something different."

One of these days, I would like you to walk around your office and write down a list of all the jobs that your fellow co-workers would love to be doing rather than working for your company. Most of them will be happy to oblige; very few will say they are satisfied with the way things are. In fact, I once read that 67% of all individuals would quit their job today if given the right opportunity.

If that' so, why aren't they creating their own opportunity?

The answer is "golden handcuffs." Managers and business owners just love golden handcuffs. These are the comforts of a job—the money, the seniority, the benefits—that keep employees at a company whether they like the job or not. Such an excellent stranglehold ensures employee retention. I am as guilty as any business owner in that I want my employees to be financially driven because it makes good business sense. If they have bills to pay, they have to sell!

But when we stay in a job that we don't really want to be in, each day we dig our selves deeper into a well of comfort. We financially strap ourselves into positions that we find hard to get out of. For example, one might not risk starting a new career or a business because of the stability offered by a current position. Even if the position is not satisfying on a personal level, we stay "handcuffed" to the job because of the "golden" comforts it provides.

Golden handcuffs have two sides. On one side, they drive us to build more wealth, because we have to live up to the standards we have thus far created. But we become accustomed to a certain lifestyle that gets too hard to remove ourselves from, so on the other side, golden handcuffs tie us to jobs we dislike so that we can maintain that lifestyle.

You'll often hear phrases like, "I can't quit my job to do that. I have bills to pay!" "What about my kids? I have to feed, clothe, and educate them, don't I?" "And what about my car payment?" "And what about . . . what about . . . what about . . . ?" Each "and what about" is a link in the chain that binds us tighter to the career we are in.

How do we break away from golden handcuffs?

Here is a list of things you can do to ensure that your ultimate dream job steps out of your dreams and into reality!

Develop a time portfolio—Write down how you spend your

time each week. Include what percentage of your waking hours is devoted to your work, spouse, family, friends, leisure, and anything else that takes a significant amount of your time. Why is this important? Well, it's like the twenty-dollar bill you start out with at the beginning of the day. You spend a little on coffee, a little on a newspaper. You grab a bagel. You buy lunch instead of bring it. In the afternoon you get thirsty, so you buy a soda. Then a candy bar. By the end of the day, you have no money left because you nickel-and-dimed it away. Don't nickel-and-dime your time away. Tally your time to see where you spend most of it. Start allocating a given amount of time each day to investigating and preparing for your ultimate job. This small daily investment of your time will add up to substantial preparation for your move.

Set aside some money for your getaway—I know you have probably heard this before, but it works. Set up a savings account at the bank. Think of it as your "career-move account." When you get your paycheck, pay yourself before you pay your bills. Over time, the money in your career-move account will compound to the point where you have enough money to venture out on your own. A rule of thumb is to have saved enough money to keep up your lifestyle and pay your bills for at least six months or up to a year. It might take some advance planning, but persistence pays off!

Control your impulse buys—Don't nickel-and-dime your future away. Every time you have an impulse to spend some money, no matter how small the amount, picture yourself in the job you want. Then run, don't walk, to an ATM or the bank and put the money you were about to spend into your career-move account.

Make purchases based on your end result—Every time you

have to make a money-spending decision that may affect any aspect of your life—such as the purchase of a home, having another child, or choosing an educational path—remind yourself of your dream job. Then, do the Ben Franklin approach to life management. Write down on a sheet of paper the pros and cons of your options. This approach will help you to decide where your money is best spent. You might see that you have to put off your ultimate dream job for a little longer, or you might see that it will actually get you the other things faster.

No debt!—You have a greater chance of having your ultimate dream job if you don't owe money! You have heard it before and I will say it again. Get out of debt! Once you get out, stay out!

THINK & ACT LIKE A WINNER

The secret to productive goal setting is in
establishing clearly defined goals, writing them down,
and then focusing on them several times a day
with words, pictures, and emotions
as if we've already achieved them.

~ Denis Waitley

Six Secrets of Success

1. There really are no secrets of success.
Success is for everyone!

2. Your life becomes better
only when you become better.

3. There is no success without sacrifice.

4. Success is achieved in inches, not miles.

5. The greatest enemy of tomorrow's success
is today's success.

6. No advice on success works unless you do.

THINK & ACT LIKE A WINNER

twenty • one

Clean Up
Your Mess...
If You Want Success

A mess is anything that keeps you distracted from success.

How many of you have come home from work in a relatively good mood, only to find yourself walking in the door and finding a mess? As you look around yourself, you notice one thing after another that needs your attention. Slowly, your good mood turns into frustration, and sometimes even anger.

Has this ever happened to you at work as well? You start off your day packed with energy and ready to go. You get to the office and see that the piles on your desk have grown overnight. You start attacking them, when one person after another comes in and interrupts you. Your phone starts ringing, and as soon as you hang it up, it rings again. Stress kicks in as you realize you're not going to meet your deadline. You find yourself slowly sinking into a pit of despair.

What a mess!

In order to be highly successful and achieve high performance, you can't have messes that keep you distracted from being your best. Think about it. How does it feel when the things on your "to-do list" are never done? What do you feel like when you have a difficult issue with a co-worker and it's never been resolved? What state of mind are you in when you know you are five months behind on balancing your checkbook? Remember, a mess is anything that distracts you from success.

Let me give you some examples of messes: a dirty car, late bills, poor relationships, a jumbled filing system, a messy house, being behind on sales quotas, not fulfilling community responsibilities, a disorganized garage. These are all examples of messes that slowly eat away at your mental health. Of course, we always tell ourselves that we will take care of things later, but some of us have so many messes to clean up that we don't even know where to begin!

A big part of being successful is feeling free of mess and disorganization. Think of the mental and physical response that you feel when your immediate to-do list is done. Wow! Nothing gets better than that! Many experience higher energy, increased thought processes, and higher self-esteem. You tend to enjoy life more when you get done the things you want to get done.

Many of the audiences that I speak to around the country tell me that they want to make more money, be more successful, and get ahead, but many share that they have a feeling of being overwhelmed. "How do I get it all done?" is a common theme among them.

I understand what they mean. Just when we accomplish one task, it seems as if two more have been added to our lists.

Let me share with you something that happened at my house. One aspect of success to me is being a good father and husband. But my house, with two small kids around it, tends to get messy. Things are misplaced and displaced. Dishes seem to be everywhere except in the kitchen. The floor sees more dirty clothes than the hamper.

As I said, I want to be a good husband and a good dad. Yet I used to come home, walk in the door, and immediately start yelling. I couldn't help it. Stuff would be everywhere! I'd usually spend such evenings saying things like, "Can't you see this?" "Why can't you finish the job?" "What smells?" "What happened in here?" "Put your stuff away."

All that yelling put me and my family in a bad mood. I found myself not doing the things that I like, my wife certainly did not think I was behaving in an exemplary fashion, and my kids thought I was a downright slave driver.

How could that type of behavior possibly have helped me and my mental outlook of being more successful in my personal and professional life?

Many of us feel that way all day, everyday. Why? Because we run from one mess to the next. Once we finish one task, another is waiting. When that's done, there's another. The thing we cleaned up last week needs cleaned up again this week. It is a vicious cycle that leaves many of us in a bad mood, and it promotes lack of creativity because we have no time to think or explore. Instead, we are overwhelmed with messes.

Having a dirty house is something that really irritates me. It drains me of feeling free and happy. It does not give me a sense of relaxation and joy. It only distracts me.

So what was my solution? There were five possibilities:

1. I could clean it.

2. My wife could clean it.

3. My oldest daughter could clean it.

4. My youngest daughter could clean it.

5. An outside expert could clean it.

Now let's inspect the reality of the circumstances.

1. I don't like cleaning the house! It is not one of my favorite chores. I would rather be doing something else. I want it cleaned, but I'm not motivated enough to clean it myself.

2. My wife is a great wife and a good doctor, yet (bless her heart) she is a mess. She is very disorganized and has no desire to be a neat freak. She would also rather be doing other things than cleaning the house. I have tried to change her ways, but I've learned firsthand that we cannot change others—all we can do is change ourselves. My wife likes having a clean house too. It also makes her feel good. But she's not good at keeping it clean, and she also has very little motivation to change that.

3. My oldest daughter is one of the reasons why our house is a mess! But she can't clean it; she is a kindergartner and isn't old enough to maintain the house.

4. The same is true of my youngest daughter.

5. The only practical solution to having a clean house, and feeling free and happy that it would be clean, was to hire an outside expert to do it.

THINK & ACT LIKE A WINNER

When people we know have a cleaning person come to their house, most of us think, "Oooh, they must be rich! They have someone to clean their house!" Yet that's not necessarily the case, at least not with us. Sometimes I want to hang a sign out in front of our house that says, "No, we are not wealthy; we just don't want to live like pigs!"

To be more successful, I have to realize that I am not always the best person to do the job. By hiring someone to help us maintain a clean house, I finally took care of one of those things that used to overwhelm me. I come home now and stay in a better mood, and we are all glad about that!

How do you feel after you have completed a project? I feel great! I feel free! I feel tension slip out of my muscles! After the garage is cleared out and organized, I stand there and look at it, proud of my accomplishment. The feeling continues throughout the week. When the house is clean, I sit on the couch and say to my wife, "Now doesn't this feel great?" When the bills are paid, my desk is clean, the grass is cut, and the car is washed, I feel great!

The feeling I get when I am organized and on top of things is how I want to feel every day. Sometimes life tends to wear us down. We run from one mess to another, never getting ahead. We have pressures at work and home. It seems like a never-ending cycle of messes. But we can clean up our messes. We can get tasks completed and feel on top of things. How?

Realize that you are not qualified to do everything—Think of yourself as running a million-dollar company. In fact, you do! If you add up the amount of money you will make over your lifetime, you will see that you will make a million dollars or more. Running a million-dollar company, we would hire people who are qualified to do our accounting, set up and maintain our computing environment, or perform our maintenance duties. Too many of us think that we will be able to get our messes cleaned up ourselves, when in reality we might be the worst candidate for the job. When you find competent people around you to do the things that they are qualified to do, they help you do what you do best.

Delegate! Delegate! Delegate!—Successful people know when it is time to delegate projects. If you are overwhelmed with tasks, pass on the responsibility for completion to someone whom you think will do the job well. That doesn't mean you give up responsibility for the task, just the responsibility to complete the task yourself. Accept that when you delegate a task, the person to whom you delegate will probably not do it the same way that you would have. This can be a problem for many people. Rather than accepting someone's aid, they put off a task because they believe they are the only person who can do it right. Don't fall into that trap. Capable assistance is available if you look for it.

Do something about it!—A mess adds to stress if you don't do something about it. Resolve that if you haven't cleaned up your messes within a month, chances are that you probably won't do it at all. And unlike teeth, messes don't go away when you neglect them; they pile up and get messier until you take action. Nip them in the bud! Either do them or, if you know in your heart that you have no desire to do them, find a capable other who will get them done for you. Don't be afraid to spend money, either. I know how to make an extra dollar, but I don't know how to get myself motivated to go down and clean out the basement. Your hard-earned money is well spent if you can be free of your messes and get on with your life.

Be creative in how you pay others for their assistance—Many people don't have their messes cleaned up because they think they can't afford it. Not true! You don't have to hire a professional cleaning service or lawn company. You don't need to consult a professional organizer or family counselor. Look around you. There are many people you know who like to do certain tasks and are good at them. You have skills, too. Perhaps you can barter. Another inexpensive way to get a mess cleaned up, and help out a student at the same time, is to hire a high-school kid who is looking to earn a buck. You can move beyond the mayhem of mess and onward to success!

Self-Management Tips

- *Start organizing NOW!*

- *Eliminate clutter to gain more time, money, energy, and peace of mind.*

- *Write down your goals for all the areas of your life.*

- *Break down projects into small tasks. Work on the difficult tasks first.*

- *Be honest about your needs. Set your boundaries and let people know what they are.*

- *Learn to say "no" without excuse or embarrassment.*

- *Try to function effectively instead of perfectly.*

~ Shari Hudson

THINK & ACT LIKE A WINNER

INDEX

I N D E X

INDEX

About the Author

Rob Wilson is a master motivator and frequent speaker on personal success. Rob began his speaking career after graduating from Drake University. He has appeared throughout the country helping men and women achieve higher levels of success.

Rob is the owner of a highly successful seminar company... A Million Miles of Motivation llc. Which was started to help individuals stay focused and motivated to achieve greater success in their business career.

Rob lives in Des Moines, Iowa with his beautiful wife and two adorable children.